TGC THE GOSPEL COALITION

THE
GOSPEL OF
LUKE
FROM THE OUTSIDE IN

DAVID MORLAN

EDITED BY D.A. CARSON

LifeWay Press®
Nashville, Tennessee

Published by LifeWay Press® • © 2013 The Gospel Coalition

ISBN: 9781415877951

Item: 005558760

Dewey Decimal Classification: 224.92

Subject Headings: BIBLE. N.T. LUKE \ CHRISTIAN LIFE \ EVANGELISTIC WORK

Unless otherwise noted, all Scripture quotations are taken from The Holy Bible, English Standard Version copyright © 2001 by Crossway, a publishing ministry of Good News Publishers. Used by permission. All rights reserved. Scriptures marked HCSB are taken from the Holman Christian Standard Bible®, Copyright 1999, 2000, 2002, 2003 by Holman Bible Publishers. Used by permission.

To order additional copies of this resource, order online at www.lifeway.com; write LifeWay Small Groups: One LifeWay Plaza, Nashville, TN 37234-0152; fax order to 615.251.5933; or call toll-free 1.800.458.2772.

Printed in the United States of America
Adult Ministry Publishing
LifeWay Church Resources
One LifeWay Plaza
Nashville, TN 37234-0152

PRODUCTION TEAM

WRITER:
DAVID MORLAN

EDITORIAL PROJECT LEADER:
BRIAN DANIEL

ART DIRECTOR:
JON RODDA

DESIGNER:
BRIAN MARSCHALL

EXECUTIVE EDITOR:
COLLIN HANSEN

GENERAL EDITOR:
D. A. CARSON

CONTENT EDITORS:
BRIAN GASS, JULIANA DUNCAN

PRODUCTION EDITOR:
MEGAN HAMBY

EXECUTIVE PRODUCER:
BEN PEAYS

VIDEO PRODUCER & EDITOR:
TIM COX

VIDEO DIRECTOR:
TIM COX

DIRECTOR, ADULT MINISTRY:
FAITH WHATLEY

DIRECTOR, ADULT MINISTRY PUBLISHING:
PHILIP NATION

CONTENTS

ABOUT THE GOSPEL COALITION

The Gospel Coalition is a fellowship of evangelical churches deeply committed to renewing our faith in the gospel of Christ and to reforming our ministry practices to conform fully to the Scriptures. We have become deeply concerned about some movements within traditional evangelicalism that seem to be diminishing the church's life and leading us away from our historic beliefs and practices. On the one hand, we are troubled by the idolatry of personal consumerism and the politicization of faith; on the other hand, we are distressed by the unchallenged acceptance of theological and moral relativism. These movements have led to the easy abandonment of both biblical truth and the transformed living mandated by our historic faith. We not only hear of these influences, we see their effects. We have committed ourselves to invigorating churches with new hope and compelling joy based on the promises received by grace alone through faith alone in Christ alone.

We believe that in many evangelical churches a deep and broad consensus exists regarding the truths of the gospel. Yet we often see the celebration of our union with Christ replaced by the age-old attractions of power and affluence, or by monastic retreats into ritual, liturgy, and sacrament. What replaces the gospel will never promote a mission-hearted faith anchored in enduring truth working itself out in unashamed discipleship eager to stand the tests of kingdom-calling and sacrifice. We desire to advance along the King's highway, always aiming to provide gospel advocacy, encouragement, and education so that current- and next-generation church leaders are better equipped to fuel their ministries with principles and practices that glorify the Savior and do good to those for whom He shed His life's blood.

We want to generate a unified effort among all peoples—an effort that is zealous to honor Christ and multiply His disciples, joining in a true coalition for Jesus. Such a biblically grounded and united mission is the only enduring future for the church. This reality compels us to stand with others who are stirred by the conviction that the mercy of God in Jesus Christ is our only hope of eternal salvation. We desire to champion this gospel with clarity, compassion, courage, and joy—gladly linking hearts with fellow believers across denominational, ethnic, and class lines.

Our desire is to serve the church we love by inviting all our brothers and sisters to join us in an effort to renew the contemporary church in the ancient gospel of Christ so that we truly speak and live for Him in a way that clearly communicates to our age. As pastors, we intend to do this in our churches through the ordinary means of His grace: prayer, the ministry of the Word, baptism and the Lord's Supper, and the fellowship of the saints. We yearn to work with all who seek the lordship of Christ over the whole of life with unabashed hope in the power of the Holy Spirit to transform individuals, communities, and cultures.

THE GOSPEL OF LUKE: FROM THE OUTSIDE IN

INTRODUCTION

The Gospel of Luke is one of four Gospels (Matthew, Mark, Luke, and John) that together comprise the first four books of the New Testament. These books are ancient biographies of Jesus that recount His life, death, and resurrection. To have a single biography of an ancient historical figure is considered a treasure by historians, but to have four of them is totally unprecedented. Indeed, we know more about Jesus than we do anyone else in antiquity. Each Gospel provides a portrait of Jesus which together gives us all we need to know in order to make important life decisions about who Jesus is and what it means to follow Him.

This study will focus on the Gospel of Luke, which is a stunning portrait of Jesus, the Son of God. Luke believes his book is the most important narrative we could ever read and invites his readers to witness His life, death, and resurrection and be transformed as a result. This is a book that presents the reader with an accurate account of Jesus but also a pathway to get to know Him personally. It is a book that calls the reader to repentance and to reorient their relationship with God through having Jesus reside at the very center.

In this story we see the life of Jesus on display and His mission in action. It starts with the circumstances around His birth and the birth of His cousin, John. We learn about Jesus' mother, Mary, and her response to the news of the coming King and the surprising role she will play in it. In this book we get a glimpse of a twelve-year-old Jesus who reminds His parents who His *real* Father is. We witness Jesus follow the lead of the Holy Spirit, preach with conviction the coming kingdom of God, and boldly direct His ministry toward a cross. It is in the Holy City that Jesus would confront not just the rulers of His day, but also the ancient foes of sin, death, and the Devil. On a hill outside of this city, Jesus would do what He came to do—die for the sins of the world. We learn that Jesus not only died, but rose from the dead to the shock of even His closest followers. This is a book about Jesus, and Luke desires all who read his Gospel to encounter God's Son for who He really is.

There are many vital themes in Luke's Gospel that are very important to understanding the whole of his message. Yet, there is a pattern in Jesus' ministry in Luke's account that we will pay particular attention to in this study: Luke highlights the gospel of Jesus going from the outside in. This theme is particularly important to point out because studying the Bible with other Christians can have an insular effect and cause a group to be inwardly focused. Luke's Gospel does *not* do that, and in this study we will show the "outside in" theme as a way to challenge Christians with the transformative work of the gospel in the lives of those considered to be "outsiders."

From start to finish Luke articulates Jesus' story as accessible to the unknowns, the outcast, the lost, and the hopeless. Jesus told the story of the stunning embrace of the returned prodigal son and the embittered response of his "righteous" brother. In doing so, Jesus shows that He desires both the irreligious and the very religious to turn to Him in repentance. We see Jesus' invitation to Zacchaeus—the hated tax collector who was eavesdropping on Jesus from the outside—and the grumbling response of the crowd on the inside: "He has gone in to be the guest of a man who is a sinner." In Luke's Gospel we witness Jesus look with compassion on a reviled, yet repentant criminal hanging on the cross next to His. In spite of it being the last moments before His death, Jesus took time to give the criminal an astonishing promise—a scandal that remains today. Jesus constantly challenged the "insiders" in Israel by highlighting "outsiders" being transformed by the gospel. He desired transformation in both camps.

This theme of the "outside in" starts as early as when the barren couple, Elizabeth and Zechariah, received word that prayers for a son, long since thought to be unanswered or forgotten, had in fact been heard by God. The story continues when Elizabeth's cousin Mary celebrated the fact that God had chosen her, a poor and lowly girl, to be the bearer of His Son. This good news caused her to rejoice in the great reversal that God had lifted up those of humble estate and that those who appeared on the inside tract of God's favor are "scattered," "brought down," and "sent away empty." This theme resumes after Jesus' wilderness experience when He was led by the Spirit to bring the good news into His hometown. A message that was widely accepted outside His hometown was bitterly rejected by insiders as they sneered, "Is not this Joseph's son?" As Jesus' ministry continued, Luke was careful to point out that Jesus' desire was not just to call sinners, but to call sinners to *repentance* (see Luke 5:32). That is, His hope is to see sinners actually respond and find reconciliation with God. As a result, this return to God by outsiders causes insiders to reevaluate the biblical story and examine what the foundation of their relationship with God *ought* to be.

This "outside in" theme is evident in Luke's narrative, but when one looks to Luke and his audience, this theme is reinforced. Luke knew what it was like to be on the outside of God's people and sympathizes with outsiders by doing little things such as translating religious terms like "scribe" into more accessible terms like "lawyer." As an educated urban Gentile, he would have been familiar with the local synagogue. Indeed, based on his understanding of the Hebrew Scriptures, he must have listened in as an outsider for years. However, growing up he would have learned the limits of his access to the God of Abraham, Isaac, and Jacob— being included in the great story of God's people was impossible for someone like him. Yet, to great delight, the message of Jesus changed that for Luke. Jesus' good news moved Luke from the "outside in" and against all odds transferred him into a full-fledged member of God's community—sons of Abraham can indeed be called out by God from the stones (see Luke 3:8; 19:9). Also consider the recipient of Luke's Gospel, Theophilus. His title "Most Excellent" hints that he was likely a wealthy government official. Like Luke, he was probably an educated Gentile who may have been considered by the Jewish community as a god-fearer. Full inclusion, however, was never going to be possible for him until Jesus changed that for Theophilus. The implications of the message of Jesus in Luke's Gospel directly impact those who are on the outside looking in. Conversely, it is a message deeply challenging to "insiders" and is designed to reveal cracked foundations upon which many have built their relationship.

I envision four main areas of growth in this study of Luke's Gospel. Luke's first audience who read his Gospel understood it to be a biography of Jesus. Jesus is the main character of this book and everything in it is meant to show us some aspect of who He is. Jesus is the singular person we are meant to truly encounter by reading this narrative. In Luke 24, Jesus says that we don't understand the Old Testament unless we read it pointing to Him. So too, Luke, writes this Gospel to display the beauty, strength, and salvation ultimately found in Jesus of Nazareth. We are to read our own lives, even the history of this world, through the lens of the life, death, and resurrection of Jesus.

The second area of growth is that Christians who participate in this study will experience a "Peter and Cornelius" moment in which they, like Peter, are awakened to God's Spirit at work in unlikely places (see Acts 10). Luke's special emphasis on the poor, sinners, and women shows surprising developments in groups of people who didn't fit the mold of what most believed God's people ought to look like. Hopefully this will cause an increasing confidence in the power of the gospel through the work of the Holy Spirit. Jesus has done and will do surprising works in breaking barriers that many believers may feel are shatterproof. Seeing this happen will increase confidence in the power of the gospel to transform the most unlikely candidates.

The third area of growth is combating our tendency as believers toward an insular sort of Christianity. The hope is that Jesus' challenge will ignite Christians toward a robust evangelicalism in which the gospel is unleashed, mission is engaged, and the Christian's self-understanding is refined. When the gospel transforms those on the outside, it causes Christians on the inside to reform and rediscover the gospel afresh.

Finally, I hope that the results of this study will be individuals coming to understand who Jesus really is for the first time and to respond in repentance and faith. In the context of the study groups, there may be a handful of curious seekers engaging the gospel who are convicted by the Spirit of their sin, and will trust in Jesus. The hope is that many will experience what Jesus described as "repentance and forgiveness of sins," and cherish the embrace of our loving Father who pronounces those once dead to now be alive. Moreover, that Christians would answer Luke's challenge and be agents of the gospel in the lives of those *outside* of the study group: unbelieving friends, co-workers, and neighbors. This study should foster relationships to be formed so that non-Christians will have an authentic encounter with the gospel of Jesus.

ABOUT THIS STUDY

The format of this short book is fairly straightforward. Begin by reading the **Introduction**, which will orient you to the text and connect the text with the broader context of Luke's narrative.

Second, read the **Text** itself. This is, of course, the most important part of the study. Indeed, if you skip or even skim the text, then the other elements of the format lose their power. You need to read the text carefully and prayerfully if you hope for this group experience to have an impact.

Third, read the **Commentary**, which will be an explanation of the text and will help point out important themes in the narrative. You will also find devotional questions to consider in the sidebar.

After this is a **Heads Up** section that will address a difficult issue in the text or perhaps address a tension that the text brings up which may be discussed in group. This short section will not "solve" the problem, but will address it in such a way that you are not overly distracted from the main themes. Once these four have been read (presumably on your own before you meet with your small group), you are now ready for your group discussion.

The group discussion begins with a **Warm-Up Question** designed to get everyone in the group thinking about certain concepts of the passage, but in a way that is accessible to those who might be new to the group or who haven't done the reading.

VIDEO AND TRANSITION

From there we move to the **Group Discussion** that will get everyone into the text and engaging Luke's message. These questions start out as observational in nature (what does the text actually say?) and then transition to interpretation (what does the text mean?), and finally application (how can the text work in my life?).

The Wrap is the close of the group time. Spend about ten minutes reiterating the bullet points and sharing prayer requests before closing in prayer.

At the end is a **Take Home** component that will push the group members to put "flesh" on the discussion and apply it during the week. Recapping this section will be an important way to begin the group discussion the following week.

ACKNOWLEDGMENT

Please note that this study does not cover everything that Luke has for us in his beautiful Gospel. There are only twelve sessions in this study to fit within a normal Bible study semester and there are twenty-four chapters in Luke. So while I will endeavor to fill in some gaps in the narrative in the study sections, there will nevertheless be important parts of Luke's story that we will skip over due to the limitations of this study.

Finally, when I started working on this short book, I was explaining to my wife the peculiar movement of the Gospel in Luke's account. During my description, she stopped me and said, "Dave, it sounds like Luke is taking the gospel from the outside in." I looked at her and thought to myself, "That is indeed what Luke is doing!" I am grateful to her for capturing this major theme in Luke's Gospel and for giving me time to write this study during "off-hours" given a demanding deadline.

JESUS AND THE CERTAINTY OF GOD

As we begin Luke's Gospel we will discover something important about how he compiled this account: he used the accounts of eyewitnesses of Jesus' ministry. Understanding Luke's use of eyewitness accounts in this narrative is very important in order to understand his writing perspective. One of the great advantages of having eyewitness accounts is that an eyewitness not only recalled what actually happened, but also had time to reflect on why it happened. In other words, an eyewitness was not only able to provide a historical reconstruction of events (as vital as that was), but also to look back and ruminate on the real meaning of those events.

Having eyewitness accounts means Luke is not only able to provide us with a wooden historical account of the Jesus movement, but also to interpret for us what theological significance surrounds these historical events. In this way, Luke will show himself to be a valuable guide in understanding the historical and theological importance of Jesus.

LUKE 1:1-4

¹ Inasmuch as many have undertaken to compile a narrative of the things that have been accomplished among us, ² just as those who from the beginning were eyewitnesses and ministers of the word have delivered them to us, ³ it seemed good to me also, having followed all things closely for some time past, to write an orderly account for you, most excellent Theophilus, ⁴ that you may have certainty concerning the things you have been taught.

COMMENTARY

When we buy a book today, we have the freedom to flip through it in order to get a sense of the whole. In the Greco-Roman world, however, one could not just peruse quickly through a scroll. This made the first few lines of any book very important because it needed to orient the reader as to what the book was about. The beginning of Luke's Gospel does a similar thing. He helps us right away by stating what he is intending to do with this Gospel: to write an "orderly account" of the events surrounding the Person and work of Jesus.

Luke acknowledges from the very beginning that others have tried to put together a narrative of the ministry of Jesus. This means that Luke was writing after Jesus had already ascended to the Father and when the mission of the church was in full swing. Luke is concerned about putting together an account of the ministry of Jesus that uses all the "eyewitnesses" still available. Eyewitnesses referred to individuals who actually followed Jesus during His ministry and interacted with Him personally (see Acts 1:21-22). Luke assures his readers that he has "followed all things closely" and is therefore qualified to pen an account of Jesus that can be trusted. This will not be a lightweight account of Jesus, but rather one that has been painstakingly researched and double-checked with the evidence available to Luke.

He has confidence he can do this because these events had already been "accomplished." That is, Luke is concerned about things that had actually happened in history concerning Jesus. There is an important distinction between events that just "happened" and events that were *"accomplished"* (perhaps a better word would be "fulfilled"). God had accomplished these things done among them! It is clear that these events were a fulfillment of what God had been up to in the history of the world. Jesus was a fulfillment of what God was doing with Israel and was a fulfillment of what God was doing through the Hebrew Scriptures. As Jesus pointed out in Luke 24:44, "everything written about me in the Law of Moses and the Prophets and the Psalms must be fulfilled."

The story Luke writes is arranged in such a way that it communicates the core meaning and message of Jesus. By "orderly account," Luke is not primarily concerned with a chronology of Jesus' ministry—though there is a basic time line that he is following in line with Mark and Matthew's Gospels—rather, Luke is more concerned that his reader "gets" who Jesus really is. Luke arranged the narrative in such a way that the reader would have to come face to face with Jesus and be compelled to make decisions about Him along the way. Is Jesus really unique among all humans who have ever lived? Is Jesus really the Son of God? If so, what does that mean for each person who reads and understands this?

The introduction style Luke uses is very interesting and lets us know about his intended readership. This is an introduction that could be read by anyone, Christian or non-Christian, and its skillful construction would communicate to an educated reader that what is to come is a thoughtful and well-researched account. The way Luke writes is sophisticated and yet not so uppity that the average reader would be lost. Luke is convinced that the message he writes will be the most important message the reader will ever receive, and he crafts his introduction so that it catches everyone's attention, regardless of religious or educational background.

Luke is writing this narrative to a particular person, Theophilus. This name means "God lover." Scholars have disagreed on who this person was, and whether or not he was even a Christian. Some believe that he had heard about Jesus and was intrigued by Him, but needed more information before committing to Him. Other scholars believe he was a young disciple of Jesus who wanted to grow, and commissioned Luke to research and write an account of Jesus so he could do just that. Regardless of who Theophilus was, he was likely asking questions such as, "Could Jesus have *really* died and risen from the dead for me? If so, what difference does it make in my life?" While there has been a debate throughout church history as to the exact identity of this person, it is clear that the intended reader is someone interested in learning more about who Jesus is and desires to know the meaning of His life, death, and resurrection.

Luke says that he will provide for Theophilus something that is very difficult to

You are the person Luke wrote for, and you are faced with these same questions about Jesus. How do you answer them now? This is a great time and place to be honest.

Which reader are you: the one who needs more information about Jesus, or the young disciple who wants to grow? How does it make you feel knowing that the story of Jesus is for you, no matter where you stand now?

obtain: certainty. If you are a convinced Christian or not, as you read this know Luke is offering you a sense of certainty in a world filled with uncertainty. One of the events that Luke desires to give you certainty about is the physical resurrection of Jesus. Luke recounts for us not just the more famous apostles' accounts of Jesus, but he gives a detailed account of two lesser-known followers as well. They walk with Jesus, talk with Him about His death, report of His resurrection, and listen to Him explain the significance of His activities from the Hebrew Scriptures. As Jesus departs from their presence, they are left with certainty that Jesus is alive, is indeed God's Son, and worth following. While Luke doesn't promise that all our questions can be answered, he does indicate that all of the major barriers that stand between you and a growing relationship with Jesus can be overcome.

HEADS UP!

Luke's Gospel is special-ordered for folks who are unsure what they believe or for folks questioning why they believed in the first place. As you meet with your group, get to know the other participants and learn how this Gospel can apply in their lives just as you endeavor to learn how it applies in your own.

Begin by asking the group how they responded to the questions in the margins and the commentary. Take turns answering the warm-up question below. Be sure everyone has an opportunity to respond.

WARM-UP (10:00)

When you think of Jesus, which facet of His life, death, or resurrection would you like more clarity about? Is there anything about Jesus that you have heard about, but you don't really know if it is true?

SHOW SESSION 1 VIDEO: JESUS AND THE CERTAINTY OF GOD (10:00)

Video times for all videos are approximate.

In this video, Dr. Carson emphasizes that Luke did extensive research and met with several eyewitnesses of Jesus when composing his Gospel. Luke did this to provide assurance to Theophilus, that he might have certainty of the things that had happened. As a group, discuss why Luke's record of eyewitness accounts provides assurance for believers.

GROUP DISCUSSION (20:00)

Spend the next several minutes engaging the discussion questions below. Try to avoid simple, pat answers and challenge yourself and the group to dig deeper into the truths the Gospel of Luke presents to us.

Luke wrote about events that had been "accomplished" by God. Talk about the most recent thing God accomplished in your life. How did you know it was a God thing and not just one of life's coincidences?

Notice Luke's attitude toward the message he wanted to share. What is your attitude toward sharing the story of Jesus?

At this point, do you feel like you "get" who Jesus is? As a group, list some things you know about Him.

_____

_____

_____

_____

Luke claims that his book will provide "certainty" for this reader regarding the things about Jesus he had been taught. In a world today where there is very little certainty about many things, what difference would it make if you had more certainty about Jesus—His message, life, death, and resurrection? What difference would it make in your family? In your church?

_____

_____

_____

_____

Go around the group and everyone share what you hope to gain as a result of being a part of this small-group study.

_____

_____

_____

_____

WRAP (10:00)

- In Jesus we have all the certainty we need.

- Luke's Gospel is an "orderly account." That is, it is presented after extensive research as being valid and true.

- Luke's findings represent the difference between events that have been *accomplished* and events that merely *happened*.

Close in prayer by asking God to bless each group member over the course of the week. Make time for the Take Home assignment below to enrich your experience with the Gospel of Luke.

TAKE HOME

This week's take home assignment is one about observation. This week listen intentionally at work, school, and home to different things people say about Jesus or Christianity. What are the common things people say? Is it generally positive or negative? Do you think what they are saying is true? Perhaps no one said anything about Him, if so, what do you think that means? Make note of your observation and discuss them in the study next week.

NOTES

NOTES

JESUS THE SON OF GOD AND THE SON OF MARY

After the introduction in verses 1-4, Luke's writing style changes dramatically. He no longer writes with sophisticated Greek constructions, but employs a writing style that changes the tone of his book—by doing this, Luke transports his reader into the ancient story of Israel. We are entered into an Old Testament-like narrative and are encouraged to get caught up in it if we want to be introduced to Jesus properly. We first meet the aged, long-suffering, yet faithful couple Elizabeth and Zechariah. Luke was careful to show the deep Jewish heritage of these two and their corresponding spiritual fidelity. Indeed, this couple represented the best of what Israel had to offer—a faithful remnant who did not compromise their faith in the face of mounting pressure. Their long-standing service to God, obedience to His commands, and unyielding requests for God to act once again, showed them to be righteous. Yet, like many righteous Hebrews in the past, they were left without a child and endured social and emotional turmoil as a result. In the midst of this situation, God's angel, Gabriel, appears before Zechariah with stunning news that God will, after all, give them a child. Their prayers proved effective as their waiting was at last over.

Their waiting represents the waiting done by the entire faithful remnant of Israel who had not heard directly from God since the days of the prophets hundreds of years before. The answer to the prayer of this couple was also the answer to the prayers and hopes of generations of Israelites—God was once again on the move. This child would be very special; a prophet like Elijah who God would use to bring repentance to Israel for the purpose of making "ready for the Lord a people prepared."

5 In the days of Herod, king of Judea, there was a priest named Zechariah,of the division of Abijah. And he had a wife from the daughters of Aaron, and her name was Elizabeth. 6 And they were both righteous before God, walking blamelessly in all the commandments and statutes of the Lord. 7 But they had no child, because Elizabeth was barren, and both were advanced in years.

8 Now while he was serving as priest before God when his division was on duty, 9 according to the custom of the priesthood, he was chosen by lot to enter the temple of the Lord and burn incense. 10 And the whole multitude of the people were praying outside at the hour of incense. 11 And there appeared to him an angel of the Lord standing on the right side of the altar of incense. 12 And Zechariah was troubled when he saw him, and fear fell upon him. 13 But the angel said to him, "Do not be afraid, Zechariah, for your prayer has been heard, and your wife Elizabeth will bear you a son, and you shall call his name John. 14 And you will have joy and gladness, and many will rejoice at his birth, 15 for he will be great before the Lord. And he must not drink wine or strong drink, and he will be filled with the Holy Spirit, even from his mother's womb. 16 And he will turn many of the children of Israel to the Lord their God, 17 and he will go before him in the spirit and power of Elijah, to turn the hearts of the fathers to the children, and the disobedient to the wisdom of the just, to make ready for the Lord a people prepared."

18 And Zechariah said to the angel, "How shall I know this? For I am an old man, and my wife is advanced in years." 19 And the angel answered him, "I am Gabriel. I stand in the presence of God, and I was sent to speak to you and to bring you this good news. 20 And behold, you will be silent and unable to speak until the day that these things take place, because you did not believe my words, which will be fulfilled in their time." 21 And the people were waiting for Zechariah, and they were wondering at his delay in the temple. 22 And when he came out, he was unable to speak to them, and they realized that he had seen a vision in the temple. And he kept making signs to them and remained mute. 23 And when his time of service was ended, he went to his home.

24 After these days his wife Elizabeth conceived, and for five months she kept herself hidden, saying, 25 "Thus the Lord has done for me in the days when he looked on me, to take away my reproach among people."

26 In the sixth month the angel Gabriel was sent from God to a city of Galilee named Nazareth, 27 to a virgin betrothed to a man whose name was Joseph, of the house of David. And the virgin's name was Mary. 28 And he came to her and said, "Greetings, O favored one, the Lord is with you!" 29 But she was greatly troubled at the saying, and tried to discern what sort of greeting this might be. 30 And the angel said to her, "Do not be afraid, Mary, for you have found favor with God. 31 And behold, you will conceive in your womb and bear a son, and you shall call his name Jesus. 32 He will be great and will be called the Son of the Most High. And the Lord God will give to him the throne of his father David, [33] and he will reign over the house of Jacob forever, and of his kingdom there will be no end."

[34] And Mary said to the angel, "How will this be, since I am a virgin?"

[35] And the angel answered her, "The Holy Spirit will come upon you, and the power of the Most High will overshadow you; therefore the child to be born will be called holy—the Son of God. [36] And behold, your relative Elizabeth in her old age has also conceived a son, and this is the sixth month with her who was called barren. [37] For nothing will be impossible with God." [38] And Mary said, "Behold, I am the servant of the Lord; let it be to me according to your word." And the angel departed from her.

[39] In those days Mary arose and went with haste into the hill country, to a town in Judah, [40] and she entered the house of Zechariah and greeted Elizabeth. [41] And when Elizabeth heard the greeting of Mary, the baby leaped in her womb. And Elizabeth was filled with the Holy Spirit, [42] and she exclaimed with a loud cry, "Blessed are you among women, and blessed is the fruit of your womb! [43] And why is this granted to me that the mother of my Lord should come to me? [44] For behold, when the sound of your greeting came to my ears, the baby in my womb leaped for joy. [45] And blessed is she who believed that there would be a fulfillment of what was spoken to her from the Lord."

[46] And Mary said,
"My soul magnifies the Lord,

⁴⁷ *and my spirit rejoices in God my Savior,*

⁴⁸ *for he has looked on the humble estate of his servant.*

> *For behold, from now on all generations will call me
> blessed;*

⁴⁹ *for he who is mighty has done great things for me,*

> *and holy is his name.*

⁵⁰ *And his mercy is for those who fear him*

> *from generation to generation.*

⁵¹ *He has shown strength with his arm;*

> *he has scattered the proud in the thoughts of their
> hearts;*

⁵² *he has brought down the mighty from their thrones*

> *and exalted those of humble estate;*

⁵³ *he has filled the hungry with good things,*

> *and the rich he has sent away empty.*

⁵⁴ *He has helped his servant Israel,*

> *in remembrance of his mercy,*

⁵⁵ *as he spoke to our fathers,*

> *to Abraham and to his offspring forever."*

⁵⁶ *And Mary remained with her about three months and
returned to her home.*

⁵⁷ *Now the time came for Elizabeth to give birth, and
she bore a son.* ⁵⁸ *And her neighbors and relatives heard
that the Lord had shown great mercy to her, and they
rejoiced with her.* ⁵⁹ *And on the eighth day they came to
circumcise the child. And they would have called him
Zechariah after his father,* ⁶⁰ *but his mother answered,
"No; he shall be called John."* ⁶¹ *And they said to her,
"None of your relatives is called by this name."* ⁶² *And
they made signs to his father, inquiring what he wanted
him to be called.* ⁶³ *And he asked for a writing tablet and*

wrote, "His name is John." And they all wondered. *64 And
immediately his mouth was opened and his tongue
loosed, and he spoke, blessing God. *65 And fear came
on all their neighbors. And all these things were talked
about through all the hill country of Judea, *66 and all
who heard them laid them up in their hearts, saying,
"What then will this child be?" For the hand of the Lord
was with him.*

*67 And his father Zechariah was filled with the Holy Spirit
and prophesied, saying,*
68 "Blessed be the Lord God of Israel,
    for he has visited and redeemed his people
69 and has raised up a horn of salvation for us
    in the house of his servant David,
*70 as he spoke by the mouth of his holy prophets from
    of old,*
71 that we should be saved from our enemies
    and from the hand of all who hate us;
72 to show the mercy promised to our fathers
    and to remember his holy covenant,
*73 the oath that he swore to our father Abraham, to
    grant us*
*74 that we, being delivered from the hand of
    our enemies,*
    might serve him without fear,
75 in holiness and righteousness before him all our days.
*76 And you, child, will be called the prophet of the
    Most High;*
    for you will go before the Lord to prepare his ways,
77 to give knowledge of salvation to his people
    in the forgiveness of their sins,

⁷⁸ *because of the tender mercy of our God,*
  whereby the sunrise shall visit us from on high
⁷⁹ *to give light to those who sit in darkness and in the*
  shadow of death, to guide our feet into the way
  of peace."
⁸⁰ *And the child grew and became strong in spirit,*
  and he was in the wilderness until the day of his
  public appearance to Israel.

²:¹ *In those days a decree went out from Caesar*
Augustus that all the world should be registered. ² *This*
was the first registration when Quirinius was governor
of Syria. ³ *And all went to be registered, each to his own*
town. ⁴ *And Joseph also went up from Galilee, from*
the town of Nazareth, to Judea, to the city of David,
which is called Bethlehem, because he was of the house
and lineage of David, ⁵ *to be registered with Mary, his*
betrothed, who was with child. ⁶ *And while they were*
there, the time came for her to give birth. ⁷ *And she*
gave birth to her firstborn son and wrapped him in
swaddling cloths and laid him in a manger, because
there was no place for them in the inn.

⁸ *And in the same region there were shepherds out in*
the field, keeping watch over their flock by night. ⁹ *And*
an angel of the Lord appeared to them, and the glory
of the Lord shone around them, and they were filled
with great fear. ¹⁰ *And the angel said to them, "Fear not,*
for behold, I bring you good news of great joy that will
be for all the people. ¹¹ *For unto you is born this day in*
the city of David a Savior, who is Christ the Lord. ¹² *And*
this will be a sign for you: you will find a baby wrapped
in swaddling cloths and lying in a manger." ¹³ *And*

suddenly there was with the angel a multitude of the heavenly host praising God and saying,
[14] "Glory to God in the highest,
and on earth peace among those with whom he is pleased!"

[15] When the angels went away from them into heaven, the shepherds said to one another, "Let us go over to Bethlehem and see this thing that has happened, which the Lord has made known to us." [16] And they went with haste and found Mary and Joseph, and the baby lying in a manger. [17] And when they saw it, they made known the saying that had been told them concerning this child. [18] And all who heard it wondered at what the shepherds told them. [19] But Mary treasured up all these things, pondering them in her heart. [20] And the shepherds returned, glorifying and praising God for all they had heard and seen, as it had been told them.

[21] And at the end of eight days, when he was circumcised, he was called Jesus, the name given by the angel before he was conceived in the womb.

[22] And when the time came for their purification according to the Law of Moses, they brought him up to Jerusalem to present him to the Lord [23] (as it is written in the Law of the Lord, "Every male who first opens the womb shall be called holy to the Lord") [24] and to offer a sacrifice according to what is said in the Law of the Lord, "a pair of turtledoves, or two young pigeons."

COMMENTARY

Many years ago my wife and I visited Florence, Italy, in hopes of seeing Michelangelo's magnificent sculpture, "David." When we entered the doors of the museum we hoped to see the sculpture right away—we only had one day in Florence and didn't have time to waste. Yet the museum was built in a way that did not allow for a casual "drop in" on this masterpiece. As we entered the museum we were led through various halls and rooms, which showcased beautiful pieces, just not the one my wife and I—and everyone else on the tour for that matter—had come to see. Finally, we were led to a room that was lined on both sides with unfinished Michelangelo sculptures and then to a specially designed room with a dome roof that showcased the famous sculpture. Having our anticipation heightened, we were prepared to take time and appreciate the sculpture for what it was.

In the introduction of his Gospel, Luke tells Theophilus that he will give an orderly account of the "things accomplished among us." We see in Luke's Gospel that the "things" he is talking about has to do with the Person and work of Jesus. Yet, when we begin reading Luke's narrative, we are instead introduced to Zechariah and Elizabeth! Then we are told about the events surrounding a special birth, but it is that of their son John, not Jesus. Jesus is not mentioned by name until Luke 1:31 when Gabriel told Mary what to name her coming son. Luke is saying that if we really want to know who Jesus is, it will not come about with a casual "drop in" here and there. Rather, we must first be placed in the story. We will not fully appreciate Jesus and all that God called Him to do if we do not first take into consideration the context of His birth and the foundations being laid several years before His ministry goes public.

After Elizabeth and Zechariah received a message from God about His plans for them to have a child, the same angel visited a young girl in the town of Nazareth. While Elizabeth was from a priestly line (daughter of Aaron), Mary and her husband-to-be were from the kingly line of the "house of David." God had promised David that his offspring would rule the Kingdom; yet, in those days, to be a priest or a king was the result of pure politics and military might. Indeed, Israel already had a "king of the Jews" whose name was Herod, having been appointed by the Roman authorities. Of course he had no connection to the house of David, but that did not matter in those days because the leadership was so thoroughly corrupt. Nevertheless, Mary received news from Gabriel about her role in God's plan to bring about the real King of the Jews. She was told that Jesus would have "the throne of His father David and he will reign over the house of Jacob forever" (v. 32). In response to this news, Mary connected the coming of her baby with God's faithfulness to

When is the last time God did something unusual and unexpected in your life? Were you able to connect that event to God's faithfulness like Mary did? Why or why not?

Though Mary felt her role in Jesus' story was out of the blue, we know it was God's plan all along. How does knowing that change the way you think about those people or situations in your life which seem to have just dropped in out of nowhere?

Israel: "he has helped his servant Israel, in remembrance of his mercy, as he spoke to our fathers, to Abraham and to his offspring forever" (vv. 54-55).

In these first two chapters Luke punctuates that Jesus did not arise out of a context-less situation—God didn't just choose Him from any random family or any random people; God didn't just drop Jesus in out of nowhere. Jesus was connected intimately with what God had been doing with the storied people of Israel through ages past. Indeed, the story that Luke tells about Jesus is not a new story, but rather the culmination of a story that reaches back thousands of years.

So, if the story Luke is telling connects Jesus with the story of Israel in the Old Testament, then that also means that the God connected to Jesus was the same as the One known as the Lord of Israel. The God who called Abraham and who was speaking through the ancient Hebrew prophets was the same God whose plan was unfolding in the opening scenes of Luke's narrative. Indeed a major character already at work in this chronicle is the Holy Spirit. Gabriel told Zechariah that the Holy Spirit would be at work in the life of John the Baptist—even from the womb. Elizabeth was filled with the Holy Spirit when she exclaimed to Mary, "blessed are you among women and blessed is the fruit of your womb!" Elizabeth's husband, Zechariah, was filled with the Holy Spirit when he uttered a prophecy about his son, John (see Luke 1:67-79). Ultimately we see the Holy Spirit at work in bringing about Jesus Himself, for as Gabriel told Mary, "The Holy Spirit will come upon you, and the power of the Most High will overshadow you." What Luke writes is not some revelation of a new divinity, but a revelation of the activity of the only true God.

The language of the Holy Spirit used in the conception of Jesus echoes the language reminiscent in the beginning of creation itself. Genesis 1:2 says, "And the Spirit of God was hovering over the face of the waters." The Holy Spirit was "hovering" over the deep before God's great act of creation and likewise He was "overshadowing" Mary before the great miracle of the conception of Jesus. Throughout Scripture we see the Holy Spirit as God's creative agent, and now we see Him at work not just creating the context for the preparation of Jesus, but involved in bringing about the incarnate Christ. In this way, Luke assures his readers that "the child to be born will be called holy—the Son of God" (see Luke 1:35). This previews a special relationship between Jesus and the Holy Spirit that we will see more closely as His ministry progresses. It also shows the magnitude of what the Father is doing in Jesus—it is an act on the scale of creation itself. This does not mean that Jesus was created at conception—a very important part of His teaching was that He existed with the Father before the creation of the world (see John 8:58)! Rather, it means that when He took on flesh, it impacted every facet of creation. If anyone desires to come to know the only God who is, that person must come to know Him through the face of Jesus.

If the story of Israel and the activity of the only true God come together dramatically in the Person of Jesus, what does that tell us about Him? Jesus is unique. The main way Luke shows us the absolute uniqueness of Jesus is through a comparison with John the Baptist. John is immensely important, a prophet like Elijah preparing the way for God's people; yet, Jesus is the Son of God and will rule as the Davidic King being God's Messiah. While John's conception occurs in the conventional way, Jesus' comes about through the creative work of the Holy Spirit. While John, like the Old Testament prophets before him, points to salvation, it is Jesus who actually brings salvation. During the naming of John, his father Zechariah gave his own son the role of prophet and forerunner while his attention was mostly given to the One who "raised up a horn of salvation for us in the house of his servant David" (Luke 1:69). Even as adults John admitted that his baptism was just with water while he pointed to Jesus' baptism being with "the Holy Spirit and fire" (Luke 3:15-18). By providing a comparison of John and Jesus, Luke wants us to see how truly unique Jesus is. If John, who was a great prophet of God, was not worthy to untie Jesus' sandals, what does that tell us about Jesus? If Jesus says that "among those born of women none is greater than John" and concludes, "yet the one who is least in the kingdom of God is greater than he", then what does that tell us about the importance of the Kingdom Jesus is establishing (7:28)? John was great, but Jesus was absolutely unique. Luke wants us to see Jesus for who He really is and in order to do that we must be willing to rearrange conventional categories as John was forced to do (see Luke 7:20).

We also see in these two chapters that Luke showcases the city of Jerusalem and the epicenter of Jerusalem, the temple. Jesus was but eight-days-old when He first entered Jerusalem and we see Him once again in Jerusalem as a twelve-year-old. Luke clearly desires his readers to see that Jesus had business to do in His "Father's" house which did not end when He was twelve (2:49), but would resurface in His public ministry. Indeed at a climactic point in His ministry, Luke narrates that Jesus, "set His face to go to Jerusalem" (9:51). Ultimately Jerusalem would be the direction His overall ministry would be heading. In Luke 2:24 we see Jesus' parents sacrificing in Jerusalem for their baby; their baby, however, would grow up and head back to Jerusalem as the ultimate sacrifice of which the sacrifices of the temple could only foreshadow.

Luke shows us that to understand Jesus, we must see Him in light of the activity of God in the ancient story of Israel. However, Luke not only situates Jesus within the history

As great a guy as John the Baptist was, Scripture says he was not worthy to untie Jesus' sandals. How does that impact your understanding of who Jesus was and is?

of God's people, but he also situates Jesus firmly within world history as well. As Luke notes, these events happened "in the days of Herod, king of Judea" and during the rule of "Caesar Augustus … when Quirinius was governor of Syria" (2:1-2). In chapter three, Luke begins by rooting Jesus' public ministry within world history: "In the fifteenth year of the reign of Tiberius Caesar, Pontius Pilate being governor of Judea, and Herod being tetrarch of Galilee, and his brother Philip tetrarch of the region of Ituraea and Trachonitis, and Lysanias tetrarch of Abilene." By doing this, Luke shows us that Jesus will not just impact Jewish history, but will impact the history of the world as well. Careful not to limit the impact to Israel alone, the stage is set for worldwide ramifications. Jesus is in line with the people of Israel and in the line of the Davidic king, but the borders of His kingdom will stretch to the ends of the earth (see Acts 1:8). Indeed, how Jesus will interact with the world will be as "a light of revelation to the Gentiles," which was an ancient vocation Israel had forsaken long ago (see Isa. 49:6; Luke 2:32).

HEADS UP!

You may have noticed something interesting about Jesus at the end of chapter two—Jesus was submissive to His parents. How can Jesus be subject to two sinful humans? Up to that point in the narrative, Luke made it clear that Jesus was absolutely unique as the very Son of God. Yet, in the brief description of the boy Jesus, we see Him manifesting a quality just as important as His divinity—His absolute humanity. A great mystery at the heart of the Christian faith is that Jesus is both 100% divine and 100% human at the same time. At certain points, He will express His divinity more clearly and at other points, like in Luke 2:51, we see Him as perfectly human. This ought not be a problem, but rather a mystery that leads us to worship Him who can completely sympathize with our human weaknesses (see Heb. 4:15), and yet has the divine power to restore us to a relationship with God by His blood.

WARM-UP (10:00)

Have you ever been caught up into an event or a movement that was bigger than you? Perhaps you helped in a political campaign, a protest, or served on a mission trip. If so, what was it like? How long did it last? How did it impact you?

SHOW SESSION 2 VIDEO: JESUS THE SON OF GOD AND THE SON OF MARY (10:00)

In this video, Dr. Carson explains that most Davidic kings were referred to as "sons of God," but that Jesus is the true Son of God. Mary conceived and gave birth to the true Son of God. As a group, discuss the implications of Jesus being fully human and fully God.

GROUP DISCUSSION (20:00)

Spend the next several minutes engaging in the discussion questions below. Try to avoid simple, pat answers and challenge yourself and the group to dig deeper into the truths and dialog the Gospel of Luke presents to us.

Why do you think it was important for Luke to give 31 verses of context before finally starting Jesus' story?

Scripture teaches that the Holy Spirit has "hovered" and "overshadowed" throughout time. In what circumstances have you sensed Him intimately involved in your circumstances?

Why do you think it was important for Luke to set up a comparison between Jesus and John the Baptist? How does that comparison affect the way you think about Jesus?

In this narrative we see grand biblical themes at play, and yet the way they are applied reach into the real lives and problems of regular people—a childless couple and the plight of a poor young girl. God doesn't just come in and impact humanity on some ethereal level—He comes in and engages humanity in the midst and the grind of real life. In what way do you see that God's big story can interact and intertwine with our individual lives?

Knowing that Jesus' ministry was for all the world, how does that change your perception of people across the globe?

Last week your group made a list of things you know about Jesus. What can you add in light of this week's reading? Are you starting to know Him better? In what ways?

_____

_____

_____

_____

WRAP (10:00)

- God didn't just drop Jesus into history out of nowhere. Jesus was intimately connected with what God had been doing with the people of Israel for ages.

- Jesus existed with the Father before the creation of the world. When He took on flesh, it impacted every part of creation.

- The humanity of Jesus is just as important as His divinity. Jesus is both 100% divine and 100% human.

Close in prayer by asking God to bless each group member over the course of the week. Make time for the Take Home assignment below to enrich your experience with the Gospel of Luke.

TAKE HOME

Your take home assignment is a prayer project. Pray that God would show you the uniqueness of Jesus. Ask God to show you His beauty and to point out in this passage of Scripture what ways He proves Himself to be truly matchless. If you are new to the faith this may feel like a strange assignment (it is okay if you think that!). Yet, even if at first feels like you are talking to yourself, continue to ask God to bring to mind the characteristics of Jesus this week and throughout this study of Luke's Gospel and what you can learn from them.

_____

_____

_____

JESUS
AND THE
SPIRIT

One of the most pressing issues all of us face in life (for some of us several times!) is the question, *What do I want to do with my life?* In a world filled with ever-increasing options, many of us find ourselves stuck in neutral when faced with major life decisions. In this passage we will see that Jesus Himself relied on the guiding of the Holy Spirit in His life. An important part of understanding Jesus is understanding the key role the Holy Spirit played in His ministry. The Spirit's leading was vital in Jesus' ministry. Learning to discern His leading was necessary for Jesus' disciples in His early ministry and is critical for His disciples today.

4:1 And Jesus, full of the Holy Spirit, returned from the Jordan and was led by the Spirit in the wilderness ²for forty days, being tempted by the devil. And he ate nothing during those days. And when they were ended, he was hungry. ³ The devil said to him, "If you are the Son of God, command this stone to become bread." ⁴ And Jesus answered him, "It is written, 'Man shall not live by bread alone.'" ⁵ And the devil took him up and showed him all the kingdoms of the world in a moment of time, ⁶and said to him, "To you I will give all this authority and their glory, for it has been delivered to me, and I give it to whom I will. ⁷ If you, then, will worship me, it will all be yours." ⁸ And Jesus answered him, "It is written,

'You shall worship the Lord your God,
and him only shall you serve.'"

⁹ And he took him to Jerusalem and set him on the pinnacle of the temple and said to him, "If you are the Son of God, throw yourself down from here, ¹⁰ for it is written,

'He will command his angels concerning you,
to guard you,'

¹¹ and
'On their hands they will bear you up,
lest you strike your foot against a stone.'"

¹² And Jesus answered him, "It is said, 'You shall not put the Lord your God to the test.'" ¹³ And when the devil had ended every temptation, he departed from him until an opportune time.

14 And Jesus returned in the power of the Spirit to Galilee, and a report about him went out through all the surrounding country. 15 And he taught in their synagogues, being glorified by all.

16 And he came to Nazareth, where he had been brought up. And as was his custom, he went to the synagogue on the Sabbath day, and he stood up to read. 17 And the scroll of the prophet Isaiah was given to him. He unrolled the scroll and found the place where it was written,

18 "The Spirit of the Lord is upon me,
because he has anointed me
to proclaim good news to the poor.
He has sent me to proclaim liberty to the captives
and recovering of sight to the blind,
to set at liberty those who are oppressed,
19 to proclaim the year of the Lord's favor."

20 And he rolled up the scroll and gave it back to the attendant and sat down. And the eyes of all in the synagogue were fixed on him. 21 And he began to say to them, "Today this Scripture has been fulfilled in your hearing." 22 And all spoke well of him and marveled at the gracious words that were coming from his mouth. And they said, "Is not this Joseph's son?" 23 And he said to them, "Doubtless you will quote to me this proverb, 'Physician, heal yourself.' What we have heard you did at Capernaum, do here in your hometown as well." 24 And he said, "Truly, I say to you, no prophet is acceptable in his hometown. 25 But in truth, I tell you, there were many widows in Israel in the days of Elijah, when the heavens were shut up three years and six months, and a great famine came over all the land, 26 and Elijah was sent to none of them but only to Zarephath, in the land of Sidon, to a woman who was a widow. *27* And there were many lepers in Israel in the time of the prophet Elisha, and none of them was cleansed, but only Naaman the Syrian."

28 When they heard these things, all in the synagogue were filled with wrath. *29* And they rose up and drove him out of the town and brought him to the brow of the hill on which their town was built, so that they could throw him down the cliff. *30* But passing through their midst, he went away.

31 And he went down to Capernaum, a city of Galilee. And he was teaching them on the Sabbath, *32* and they were astonished at his teaching, for his word possessed authority. *33* And in the synagogue there was a man who had the spirit of an unclean demon, and he cried out with a loud voice, *34* "Ha! What have you to do with us, Jesus of Nazareth? Have you come to destroy us? I know who you are—the Holy One of God." *35* But Jesus rebuked him, saying, "Be silent and come out of him!" And when the demon had thrown him down in their midst, he came out of him, having done him no harm. *36* And they were all amazed and said to one another, "What is this word? For with authority and power he commands the unclean spirits, and they come out!" *37* And reports about him went out into every place in the surrounding region.

38 And he arose and left the synagogue and entered Simon's house. Now Simon's mother-in-law was ill with a high fever, and they appealed to him on her behalf. *39* And he stood over her and rebuked the fever, and it left her, and immediately she rose and began to serve them.

40 Now when the sun was setting, all those who had any

who were sick with various diseases brought them to him, and he laid his hands on every one of them and healed them. ^{41} And demons also came out of many, crying, "You are the Son of God!" But he rebuked them and would not allow them to speak, because they knew that he was the Christ.

^{42} And when it was day, he departed and went into a desolate place. And the people sought him and came to him, and would have kept him from leaving them, ^{43} but he said to them, "I must preach the good news of the kingdom of God to the other towns as well; for I was sent for this purpose." ^{44} And he was preaching in the synagogues of Judea.

COMMENTARY

If you have ever been in a taxi, one of the first things you see as you slide into the back seat is the certification of the driver with his picture on it. This is important because you don't know the driver personally and yet you find yourself in the back of his car! Riding in a taxi provokes questions such as, "Is the driver heading in the right direction?" "Did he hear the address correctly?" or, "Is he going to overcharge me?" All of these anxieties arise because you don't really know who is driving the car. As Jesus begins His ministry we see Him go to some very unlikely places, have painful experiences, and meet some unsavory individuals. As we follow His journey it may be easy to ask, is Jesus' ministry heading in the right direction? Is it wise to have direct confrontation with Satan after forty days of no food; wouldn't Jesus be at His most vulnerable in that physical state? Is it smart to have a direct confrontation with His hometown friends and family; wouldn't they provide the best support base for Him and His ministry? To these questions Luke reminds his readers who is "driving" Jesus' ministry. Jesus is "full of the Holy Spirit." Jesus is "led by the Holy Spirit." Jesus is "in the power of the Holy Spirit." Jesus claimed a prophecy that, "The Spirit of the Lord was upon him." If Jesus is full of, led by, and in the power of the Spirit we can be assured that the direction of Jesus' ministry is exactly where it is supposed to be.

When have you seen a Christian making seemingly unwise decisions, only to find out it was indeed directed by the Holy Spirit? Why is it hard to imagine the Holy Spirit acting outside of what you think is best?

This is important to keep in mind because the first place the Spirit led Jesus was directly to the wilderness to be tested by Satan. As Jesus started His ministry there were no "softballs" lobbed to Him; rather He was led to a point where He was physically exhausted and then interrogated by Satan. Many other saints of the past had been tested in the wilderness and it didn't go very well for them. Yet, it is in this condition that Jesus shows us something very important about Himself: He succeeds where all others in the past had failed.

In the Old Testament, faithfulness to God was proven in the midst of testing. How Jesus responds to this testing tells us about His ability to bring about God's plan of salvation. The Devil appeared to Jesus and challenged Him saying, "If you are the Son of God then..." In each of the three tests, Jesus was prompted to "give in" to the flesh (physically by eating bread), power (by being granted kingdoms), and importance (by the means of an insidious submission to Satan). Ironically, by His not giving in to the temptation to "prove" He was the Son of God, He actually showed Himself to be the Son of God. In each case Jesus passed the test, showing His true vocation and divine Sonship. He identified with the hunger and frustration of physical weakness, and yet trusted in God's word at a time when "giving in" could have easily been justified.

Think about the last time you were tested or beaten up on by the devil. Did you stand fast, or did you give in? What temptations of Satan do you find most difficult to resist?

We read in Exodus that Israel, like Jesus here, was allowed to hunger and given an opportunity to learn to live by the Word of God. In the wilderness Israel was instructed to worship the one and only God and not to follow any other "deity." Finally, Israel was commanded not to put God to the test. In all three of these occasions Israel failed miserably. Jesus showed Himself to be truly faithful in the exact areas where there had been past failure by Israel.

Jesus' victory not only showed Him to be a faithful Israelite, but also shows what a faithful human being looks like. Interestingly, when Jesus' genealogy is recounted in Luke 3, it does not simply go back to Abraham (as it does in Matthew 1:2 which highlights the deep Jewish heritage of Jesus), rather Luke takes it all the way back to Adam (see Luke 3:38). In this way Jesus is not only representative of Israel but of all humanity. Jesus is the Son of God who was faced, like Adam, with a choice to trust in God's Word or to bite into the fruit that the Devil offers. Jesus is, as Paul described Him, a second Adam. And where Adam failed, Jesus succeeded.

As we ponder the testing of Jesus, it is important to remember Jesus' full humanity. There was a heresy that emerged in the early church that claimed Jesus only appeared to be human but in reality was not. This belief sprouted in order to explain the remarkable works of Jesus; yet, in the wilderness we see Jesus as fully human. Jesus was a real man and faced what Adam faced.

From the wilderness, Jesus was directed by the Spirit to go to His hometown, Nazareth. Jesus was back in His "home" synagogue and everyone was amazed by what they saw and heard. Jesus read a prophecy from Isaiah and said it was fulfilled immediately after His reading of it. They were astonished! And then suddenly their approval transferred into skepticism when they said, "Isn't this Joseph's son?" Saying this reminded them that Jesus couldn't possibility be all that important because He had the same humble origins as they did.

If it seems like Jesus then caused disruption in His hometown, it is because He did! Jesus immediately talked about the healing ministry of Elijah and Elisha. These past prophets had angered Israel because God healed the "wrong" kind of people through them. God used these prophets to heal the "outsiders" and doing this made the insiders in Israel furious. As Jesus referenced this point, His hometown—the ultimate insiders on Jesus, who witnessed Him grow up—became enraged. Indeed, they even wanted to kill Him. How dare He not be exactly who they thought He should be!

Jesus' interaction with His hometown demonstrates the danger of letting familiarity with Jesus serve as a substitute for actual knowledge of Him. Jesus is confrontational toward those who "think" they have Him figured out and placed neatly into a box. "Isn't this Joseph's son?" Yet those who pose this query are the very ones who need to have their foundations about Jesus reexamined altogether.

As Jesus confronted His hometown, remember that this was in the direction of the Holy Spirit. He went home in the power of the Spirit and was rejected. This is the typical pattern of the initial reaction many people have to Jesus "coming home" in the power of the Spirit. We don't like it and desire to push Him out. It is uncomfortable when Jesus comes in power and rearranges areas of our lives that are complacent and comfortable. We resist change and conviction and in reaction try to eliminate the One who is bringing the change.

Ironically, while His own neighbors and relatives didn't know who Jesus really was, evil spiritual forces knew exactly who He was. They cried out, "Ha! What have You to do with us, Jesus of Nazareth? Have You come to destroy us? I know who You are—the Holy One of God." And others yelled, "You are the Son of God!" In this section, we see Jesus' true opponent—the Devil and his minions—and we begin to see the scope of Jesus'

Have you ever felt frustrated to learn that an "outsider," someone "too far gone" has professed to know Jesus? How can you guard against that kind of hard-heartedness?

power revealed. He not only talked as if having authority and He not only claimed to fulfill prophecy, but when He talked things actually happened. Rebuking a fever or rebuking a demon made no difference—both illness and the malignant spirit obeyed the One who had authority over them.

HEADS UP!

The problem with going home is returning to people who know you or, to put it more accurately, people who may think they know you. Folks in Nazareth knew Jesus—He was the son of Joseph after all and they watched Him grow up in Joseph and Mary's household. But did they really know Him? In many years of pastoral counseling, I've noticed a reoccurring issue at the heart of many family problems: family members often do not really know each other. They may have lived together for many years and know thousands of things about each other, but during authentic communication, they realize they really don't understand each other. There is something about familiarity that is dangerous because it breeds a complacency that lures one into thinking that there is understanding when that is often not the case. When this happens, the opportunity for real understanding is gone because they have already settled for a false sense of understanding. As you continue in Luke's Gospel keep in mind our tendency to try to limit Jesus' power and influence in our lives. Remember that doing this causes us to grow complacent and reduces our ability to truly understand Him better.

WARM-UP (10:00)

Have you ever faced a significant "test" in your life? If so, what was it like? How did it turn out?

SHOW SESSION 3 VIDEO: JESUS AND THE SPIRIT (10:00)

In this video, Dr. Carson explains that all Persons of the Godhead (Father, Son, and Holy Spirit) are working together to bring about the mission that is encapsulated in the gospel. As a group, discuss why the Holy Spirit is an important part of the Trinity. Specifically, discuss how the Spirit led in the life of Jesus and how He leads in yours.

GROUP DISCUSSION (20:00)

Spend the next several minutes engaging in the discussion questions below. Try to avoid simple, pat answers and challenge yourself and the group to dig deeper into the truths and dialog the Gospel of Luke presents to us.

Luke describes Jesus' interaction with Satan in the wilderness. How do you feel about the fact that the three temptations Jesus faced were typical of what we face today? What does it prove about our identity when we don't give in to temptations?

Describe a time God used your lack in a given area to prove His sufficiency.

In this passage we see several references to Jesus and the Holy Spirit. The Holy Spirit will continue to be a major theme in this Gospel. Reread the references to Jesus and the Spirit in this chapter and then read Jesus' last words in Luke 24:49. What does this tell us about the role the Holy Spirit plays in our mission today and in having boldness?

Knowing Jesus was fully human, what avoidance tactics can you take from His wilderness experience to use next time you are being tempted?

How have you seen familiarity with Jesus turn into something negative?

WRAP (10:00)

- The Holy Spirit was "driving" Jesus' ministry. Jesus was full of, led by, and in the power of the Spirit.

- While Jesus was led to the wilderness to be tested by Satan, He showed something very important about Himself. He succeeds where all others in the past had failed.

- The Holy Spirit led Jesus to places where He was rejected. This is true for us today as well, but we sometimes resist change and conviction and in reaction reject the One who is bringing the change.

Close in prayer by asking God to bless each group member over the course of the week. Make time for the Take Home assignment below to enrich your experience with the Gospel of Luke.

TAKE HOME

Your take home assignment this week is to read what Jesus was teaching His disciples about the role of the Holy Spirit in their lives. First, read the following passages out of John's Gospel (John 14:25-26, 15:26-27, and 16:6-11). Second, answer the question: based on these passages, what function did Jesus say the Holy Spirit plays in our lives and in the broader world today?

NOTES

JESUS AND THE WORD OF GOD

In our society we are inundated by words and images vying for our attention (and money!). According to *The New York Times*, we receive between 2,000 and 5,000 messages per day! As a result—in order to keep sane—most of us try to tune out the vast majority of those messages.

While not on the scale of today's advertising onslaught, those in Jesus' day received many different messages that summoned allegiance from their hearers. Yet, despite a chorus of voices, Jesus' message began to draw a following. Not because His words were the most clever, but because His words had real power. Jesus' words had the authority of God in them.

39 He also told them a parable: "Can a blind man lead a blind man? Will they not both fall into a pit? 40 A disciple is not above his teacher, but everyone when he is fully trained will be like his teacher. 41 Why do you see the speck that is in your brother's eye, but do not notice the log that is in your own eye? 42 How can you say to your brother, 'Brother, let me take out the speck that is in your eye,' when you yourself do not see the log that is in your own eye? You hypocrite, first take the log out of your own eye, and then you will see clearly to take out the speck that is in your brother's eye.

43 "For no good tree bears bad fruit, nor again does a bad tree bear good fruit, 44 for each tree is known by its own fruit. For figs are not gathered from thornbushes, nor are grapes picked from a bramble bush. 45 The good person out of the good treasure of his heart produces good, and the evil person out of his evil treasure produces evil, for out of the abundance of the heart his mouth speaks.

46 "Why do you call me 'Lord, Lord,' and not do what I tell you? 47 Everyone who comes to me and hears my words and does them, I will show you what he is like: 48 he is like a man building a house, who dug deep and laid the foundation on the rock. And when a flood arose, the stream broke against that house and could not shake it, because it had been well built. 49 But the one who hears and does not do them is like a man who built a house on the ground without a foundation. When the stream broke against it, immediately it fell, and the ruin of that house was great."

7:1 After he had finished all his sayings in the hearing of the people, he entered Capernaum. ² Now a centurion had a servant who was sick and at the point of death, who was highly valued by him. ³ When the centurion heard about Jesus, he sent to him elders of the Jews, asking him to come and heal his servant. ⁴ And when they came to Jesus, they pleaded with him earnestly, saying, "He is worthy to have you do this for him, ⁵ for he loves our nation, and he is the one who built us our synagogue." ⁶ And Jesus went with them. When he was not far from the house, the centurion sent friends, saying to him, "Lord, do not trouble yourself, for I am not worthy to have you come under my roof. ⁷ Therefore I did not presume to come to you. But say the word, and let my servant be healed. ⁸ For I too am a man set under authority, with soldiers under me: and I say to one, 'Go,' and he goes; and to another, 'Come,' and he comes; and to my servant, 'Do this,' and he does it." ⁹ When Jesus heard these things, he marveled at him, and turning to the crowd that followed him, said, "I tell you, not even in Israel have I found such faith." ¹⁰ And when those who had been sent returned to the house, they found the servant well.

COMMENTARY

In high school I always felt sorry for substitute teachers, especially in math class. In theory they had authority over the class, but when they gave instructions or made requests, nothing ever seemed to happen. Words that came out of their mouths had no power and

Have there been
times that you
were surprised
at the words
coming out
of your own
mouth? Looking
back, what was
the condition
of your heart
at that time?

made no impact on us. Furthermore, the substitute teacher was often not prepared to teach on the topic and the rare times we did listen, the words had very little to contribute to our math skills. As we look to Jesus in this session, we discover His words are much different than those that came from other teachers in His day. Jesus shows His words to be authoritative in three different ways: they have authority based on their source; they have authority based on their trustworthiness; and they have authority based on their power to enable and accomplish a task.

This passage starts with four terrific word pictures. The section about the blind man is a lesson about discerning teachers. Jesus reminded His listeners that it is foolish to follow anyone's teaching when they themselves don't know where they are going. Even if they teach with confidence the wise listener will perceive where their teaching will lead. The next story builds on the first, and communicates that one can only go as far as the teacher himself. If you do not like the life of a Pharisee, then why would you desire to follow their teaching? You will become like one in the process. The next illustration is about finding a speck of dust in another person's eye. Jesus warns against those who are overly critical of others when they themselves are fundamentally hypocritical. Jesus understood that teachers often avoided their own brokenness by emphasizing the brokenness of others. In all three of these stories, Jesus calls our attention to the source from which words flow. If teachers are not people of integrity then what they have to say ought to be taken with extreme caution. Jesus summarizes this section by saying that eventually what is in a person will come out of a person. A healthy tree produces healthy fruit and a sick tree produces bad fruit. Likewise, when listening to teaching, one needs to be as concerned about the teacher and whether or not he or she has a life worthy to be followed, as much as one is concerned about the content of the teaching itself.

After emphasizing the source of the teaching, Jesus then turns our attention to the lasting value of the substance of teaching. As we look at Jesus' words in this passage we see that Jesus challenged the dedication of those who claimed allegiance to Him but did not base their lives on His words. Jesus had just finished His "sermon on the plain" (see Luke 6:12-45) and now warned that listening to His words but not "doing" what He says leads to disaster. Jesus believed His teaching was strong enough to serve as a solid foundation and worthy to build a life upon. Indeed, to see it another way, any foundation for one's life other than Jesus will lead to disappointment. Any other foundation would be akin to building a house on a sand foundation. Life may go well for a while but when faced with difficulty, the house would shift and eventually fall apart. Calamities come when you don't expect it. One doesn't have time to prepare for a disaster in the midst of the storm. The time of the disaster reveals one's readiness. Jesus was warning His disciples that when the difficulties of life come, one's foundation is already determined.

When is the last time you experienced growth that caused lasting change? How did you move from just having the desire to actually making the change happen?

Jesus then addressed some practical issues about how one is to follow His teaching. How can disciples do Jesus' words as He is instructing them to? This may seem like an obvious question, but many have a desire to do something and cannot muster the power and energy to do it. Jesus answers this question in two ways, and both of these are very important if we want to know how to respond to God's Word. First, the words "coming," "hearing," and "building a house" are all participles in the present tense. Jesus is urging His disciples to participate in a continuous process. "Do" is not simply a one-time, "do what I say" in the present, but rather an ongoing process that describes the daily life of a disciple. Jesus' words are not self-help, quick-fix solutions. Instead, they are words to be processed, meditated upon, and given time to shape us. What Jesus is describing is not an "overnight" extreme makeover session, but slow and steady growth that reaches into the disciple and causes lasting change. The problem the builder faced in Jesus' story was not necessarily the location of the house, but how the house was built. Did the builder take a shortcut and build on what seemed to be a solid foundation, or did he do the hard work of digging down to the bedrock? The temptation to find the quick fix did not fit with how Jesus described the authentic work of discipleship. Yet, if we don't lay a solid and deep foundation, then storms reveal our poor preparation and easily render our lives unsettled.

Secondly, we see that Jesus' words are followed because of a characteristic unique to Jesus: His words inherently have divine power to accomplish what He sets out to accomplish. When Jesus spoke, realities were changed, physicalities were altered, and things actually happened. Jesus was approached by the elders of the Jews with a request of a centurion whose servant was near death. In this story we see that the centurion understood the dynamic between words and authority. As someone who had many soldiers under his command, he knew that when he gave them an instruction, they must follow his orders. He not only had the "official" title, but he had real authority as demonstrated by the obedience of those whom he commanded.

The centurion's own power derived from his connection with the Roman Emperor. The Emperor had the power to take a life if he so desired and soldiers understood the reality of that power. Therefore, they obeyed the centurion because he was connected to that power. Likewise, the centurion respected Jesus' words because he realized that Jesus was under the command of the creator God. Yet, even as a servant of the Emperor, the

You have the opportunity to freely explore and experience the words of Jesus anytime you wish. How does your reaction to Jesus compare to the centurion's? What surprises you about his reaction?

centurion understood that Jesus possessed an even greater power—Jesus had power to create life out of death with just a word.

The centurion provides a sterling example of how one responds to the word of God. First, we see him approach Jesus with great humility. The centurion used "go-betweens" twice in this story. This was a common practice when someone of lesser standing needed to send a message to someone of higher standing. This is highly ironic because Jesus did not possess the official rank or title that the centurion did. Yet, he understood something about Jesus that even the Jewish leaders did not see. The centurion felt the same as John the Baptist—Jesus had a direct connection to God and therefore he did not feel worthy to be in His presence. Second, he responded to Jesus' word by faith. An amazing thing about the centurion's insight into Jesus was that he intuitively sensed Jesus' power despite having never met Jesus before! He had only heard about Jesus. However, based on that testimony, he had enough to know what kind of Person Jesus was and that He was Someone he could trust. This is important to note because, as we saw at the beginning of this study, Theophilus, like this centurion, had not met Jesus personally, but only had the word of eyewitnesses to verify Jesus. The response of the centurion is a great reminder to the modern reader that responding to Jesus is not based on complete revelation or having every possible question about Him answered, but rather it is based on having the right questions answered about Him in the Power of God.

Finally, we see this section end with a surprising twist: the words that Jesus marvels at are the words of the centurion. Normally people were astonished at what Jesus said, but here Jesus was astonished at what the centurion said (see Rom. 2:29). Jesus used the faith of the centurion as a stinging rebuke of Israel's faith. "I tell you, not even in Israel have I found such faith" (Luke 7:9). This ultimate outsider of Israel had greater faith than those who had the inside track to understand who Jesus really was.

HEADS UP!

While the focus of this lesson is on Jesus' words, there is also a sub-theme of grace that should not be overlooked. The centurion understood his sinful position before Jesus. Even though he did very good things and earned the respect of the community, he was keenly aware that his works could not achieve the sort of righteousness that was needed. In this way he is like other individuals we will meet in Luke's Gospel. He is like the prodigal son who declared to his Father "I am no longer worthy to be called your son" (15:19, 21), and he is like the tax collector at the temple who stands far off and says, "God, make atonement for me, a sinner!" (18:13). The centurion demonstrated the proper posture toward God: an utter awareness that we are undeserving of His salvation and, at the same time, a boldness that comes from complete trust in the power and grace of Jesus alone.

WARM-UP (10:00)

Can you remember a time when someone spoke words to you that proved deeply impactful? If so, what were they and how did it impact your life?

SHOW SESSION 4 VIDEO: JESUS AND THE WORD OF GOD (10:00)

In this video, Dr. Carson points out the emphasis the four Gospels place on Jesus' words. He says that to put Jesus' words into action is to build a stable foundation. As a group, discuss this statement and why listening to His words is so important.

GROUP DISCUSSION (20:00)

Spend the next several minutes engaging in the discussion questions below. Try to avoid simple, pat answers and challenge yourself and the group to dig deeper into the truths and dialog the Gospel of Luke presents to us.

We've all encountered highly critical people. How do you deal with them? Based on this week's reading, what could be the reason for their attitude and why is it important that you consider that before you react?

We learned in this session that Jesus' words are not self-help, quick-fix solutions. So what does it take from you to experience the kind of growth and change He promises?

Jesus was concerned that His listeners would settle for lives built on sandy foundations. What is it about building our lives on sand that is so seductive? Why is it difficult to build a house on bedrock?

Jesus never criticized His disciples for having too much faith. Rather it was always that their faith was much too small. In this story the faith of the centurion rested solely in the power of Jesus' words. In what ways do you feel your faith in Jesus shows itself to be too small?

In this passage the authority of Jesus' words did not derive from His position as teacher, but in their ability to actually get things done. Whose words do you trust in and why?

_____

_____

_____

_____

WRAP (10:00)

- Jesus' words are authoritative in three ways: they have authority based on their source; they have authority based on their trustworthiness; and they have authority based on their power to enable and accomplish a task.

- Jesus' words inherently have divine power to accomplish what He sets out to do.

- Jesus' teaching is strong enough to serve as a solid foundation and worthy to build a life upon.

Close in prayer by asking God to bless each group member over the course of the week. Make time for the Take Home assignment below to enrich your experience with the Gospel of Luke.

TAKE HOME

The focus of this week's assignment is an exercise in trust. As we have read, Jesus calls us to trust in His word. This week identify one area of your life in which you have never really trusted in Jesus before (or an area that has always been difficult to trust Jesus in). Once identified, what would it look like to trust God's Word in this area of your life?

_____

_____

_____

_____

NOTES

NOTES

JESUS AND THE
POWER
OF GOD

One of the frustrating aspects of our humanity is coming to terms with the limitations of our power. We are not really in control and occasionally things happen in our lives that remind of us this fact. Yet, for those who attached themselves to Jesus, they were beginning to understand that Jesus' power was quite different than their own.

This passage introduces us to the magnificent power of Jesus unleashed in three different ways. First, Jesus encountered an army of evil spirits who realized the inherent power of Jesus upon their first sight of the Son of God. Second, we see His power in the instant healing of a woman when all other attempts had failed. And last, we will see His power evidenced by the resurrection of a dead girl at His command. In each of these stories, we see people submit to Jesus in humility. In all three situations, the individuals acutely understood the power delineation. They knew they were powerless and that Jesus Himself was all-powerful. Jesus shows us the power of God and perhaps in this passage we will see that for many of us, our understanding of Jesus is much too tame.

26 Then they sailed to the country of the Gerasenes, which is opposite Galilee. 27 When Jesus had stepped out on land, there met him a man from the city who had demons. For a long time he had worn no clothes, and he had not lived in a house but among the tombs. 28 When he saw Jesus, he cried out and fell down before him and said with a loud voice, "What have you to do with me, Jesus, Son of the Most High God? I beg you, do not torment me." 29 For he had commanded the unclean spirit to come out of the man. (For many a time it had seized him. He was kept under guard and bound with chains and shackles, but he would break the bonds and be driven by the demon into the desert.) 30 Jesus then asked him, "What is your name?" And he said, "Legion," for many demons had entered him. 31 And they begged him not to command them to depart into the abyss. 32 Now a large herd of pigs was feeding there on the hillside, and they begged him to let them enter these. So he gave them permission. 33 Then the demons came out of the man and entered the pigs, and the herd rushed down the steep bank into the lake and drowned.

34 When the herdsmen saw what had happened, they fled and told it in the city and in the country. 35 Then people went out to see what had happened, and they came to Jesus and found the man from whom the demons had gone, sitting at the feet of Jesus, clothed and in his right mind, and they were afraid. 36 And those who had seen it told them how the demon-possessed man had been healed. 37 Then all the people of the surrounding country of the Gerasenes asked him to

depart from them, for they were seized with great fear. So he got into the boat and returned. [38] *The man from whom the demons had gone begged that he might be with him, but Jesus sent him away, saying,* [39] *"Return to your home, and declare how much God has done for you." And he went away, proclaiming throughout the whole city how much Jesus had done for him.*

[40] *Now when Jesus returned, the crowd welcomed him, for they were all waiting for him.* [41] *And there came a man named Jairus, who was a ruler of the synagogue. And falling at Jesus' feet, he implored him to come to his house,* [42] *for he had an only daughter, about twelve years of age, and she was dying.*

As Jesus went, the people pressed around him. [43] *And there was a woman who had had a discharge of blood for twelve years, and though she had spent all her living on physicians, she could not be healed by anyone.* [44] *She came up behind him and touched the fringe of his garment, and immediately her discharge of blood ceased.* [45] *And Jesus said, "Who was it that touched me?" When all denied it, Peter said, "Master, the crowds surround you and are pressing in on you!"* [46] *But Jesus said, "Someone touched me, for I perceive that power has gone out from me."* [47] *And when the woman saw that she was not hidden, she came trembling, and falling down before him declared in the presence of all the people why she had touched him, and how she had been immediately healed.* [48] *And he said to her, "Daughter, your faith has made you well; go in peace."*

[49] *While he was still speaking, someone from the ruler's house came and said, "Your daughter is dead; do not*

trouble the Teacher any more." [50] *But Jesus on hearing this answered him, "Do not fear; only believe, and she will be well."* [51] *And when he came to the house, he allowed no one to enter with him, except Peter and John and James, and the father and mother of the child.* [52] *And all were weeping and mourning for her, but he said, "Do not weep, for she is not dead but sleeping."* [53] *And they laughed at him, knowing that she was dead.* [54] *But taking her by the hand he called, saying, "Child, arise."* [55] *And her spirit returned, and she got up at once. And he directed that something should be given her to eat.* [56] *And her parents were amazed, but he charged them to tell no one what had happened.*

COMMENTARY

This passage begins with Jesus sailing across the Sea of Galilee. Immediately after Jesus stepped out of the boat, a man possessed with demons confronted Him. This was not a routine possession because this afflicted man was taken over by many demons. The demons had completely invaded his body. His existence was an extreme distortion of humanity. He wore no clothes, lived among the dead, and even chains couldn't shackle him. He was isolated from his community, and driven to madness and hopelessness.

The demons that controlled this man immediately recognized Jesus. They intrinsically knew that His power far exceeded theirs. Jesus was the "Son of the Most High God," and the demons knew that their fate rested solely in Jesus' word. The possessed man responded to Jesus' query of his name with, "Legion." The name Legion did not simply denote a large number (5,600 soldiers would constitute a legion), but the term referred to a large organized collection of soldiers who were connected to a greater army. In other words, these demons were a collection of evil spirits at war against this man, and through him against God. Yet at the sight of Jesus, they cowered and began to make the terms of their surrender.

The demons begged that He would not send them to the place of eternal destruction (abyss), but instead into a herd of pigs. Their interaction with Jesus showed that they were fully aware of what their final destiny held—yet they did not desire for the end quite yet. Their understanding of who Jesus was and what the end held for them is ironic in that Jesus' own disciples did not yet have this understanding fully. Jesus' disciples had yet to realize the depth of who this "Son of the Most High God" was and by their questions didn't understand how the "end" would play out in their lives and in Jesus' ministry. The demons, however, understood these things, but Legion's understanding did not change its death-inducing nature. Their shameless pleading revealed the selfish and life-draining nature of demonic forces—while they were highly concerned about their own imminent torment, they showed no concern about the man whose body they occupied and controlled. Yet, the observed irony of their request was that the instant Jesus granted their appeal, the demons assumed control of the pigs and caused the destruction of the pigs and themselves as well.

Jesus thoroughly and competently demonstrated His ability to overcome the dark forces that warred against God. The demons deferred to Jesus and demonstrated their subordination by utilizing the word "permit" twice; Jesus was in control and had ultimate power. The militant occupation of this poor man's life had come to an end at last. The saving act by Jesus liberated this man from the demons and liberated the geographical area from the influence of these evil forces.

Despite His redemptive presence, the Gerasene people did not want Jesus to stay and asked Him to leave their region—which He did. The liberated man desired to leave and join Jesus on His mission. However, Jesus had other plans for him. Jesus instead instructed him to stay and spread the news of all that God had done for him. This man rightly understood that the power he experienced through Jesus was the power of God, and so he thus proclaimed to the people of his community all that Jesus had done for him. Although Jesus was asked to leave, He exited with a newly converted evangelist remaining in that Gentile area. The Gerasene people were forced to grapple with the unquestioned miracle and salvation brought to one of their own.

Once again, Jesus took His gospel from the outside in. Jesus saved the outsider and directed him back into his hometown with the news of everything that had happened to him. How his community responded to his testimony remains unknown, but the initial zeal and dedication of the man to the message and Person of Jesus is certain.

In contrast to the unwelcoming request for His exit from the country of the Gerasenes, Jesus was enthusiastically welcomed by His fellow Jews. In fact, a leader of the

For many, perhaps even you, thinking about demons and darkness is uncomfortable. Yet we can't ignore their existence. How does the reality of demons make you feel? How does knowing Jesus has authority over them change your feelings on the subject?

List at least five good things Jesus has done for you and circle the things you then told people about. Who can you share your story with and what impact might it have?

synagogue rushed ahead of the crowd and fell down before Jesus begging Him to come see his only daughter who was near death. For an esteemed Jewish leader to fall before Jesus revealed his desperation. He was reduced to complete humility on behalf of his daughter. Jesus responded favorably to his heartfelt humility and began to travel toward her. Here we see that Jesus' ministry was not exclusively open to "outsiders," but to anyone who came to Him in need. Indeed, Jesus lovingly received even successful "insiders" like this synagogue leader as he was driven to Him by overwhelming need.

During His journey toward the Jewish leader's daughter, Jesus abruptly stopped and made a strange pronouncement that someone had touched Him. People surrounded Jesus and the entire crowd was pressing in on Him; yet He knew that someone has been healed through Him. Of course, Jesus knew who it was that touched Him—a woman who had an ailment for twelve years which rendered her penniless and impure. Indeed, her condition had major physical and social implications that solidified her status as an outsider. Nevertheless, she had such belief in the power of Jesus that she was certain touching His clothes would be enough for her to be healed—and she was right!

Jesus was aware that His healing power left Him, and requested for the recipient to speak up, which she did. What she hoped to be a private, personal experience of healing turned into a public pronouncement of healing to a large crowd. This woman who was unclean and out of financial resources was outed and forced to respond to her Healer in public. This potentially damaging encounter turned into a joyous reintroduction to her own people. Moreover, that an unclean woman touched Jesus should have rendered Jesus ceremonially unclean by Jewish standards. But in fact, it had the reverse effect. Instead of making Him unclean, the unclean woman who touched Him became clean!

Interestingly, Jesus' response to her was that her faith had made her well. It was not simply faith, but her faith in Jesus that made her well. It was a faith based on who He was and on His proven power—it was not a blind faith based on sentimental well-wishing. It was a real faith based on Someone worthy of such trust.

Jesus' power was again showcased in contrast to the other means of healing in that day. Jesus could heal when all others could not. And Jesus expected no remittance for His services—she was simply instructed to "go in peace." The word for peace in the New Testament is not how we commonly understand it today, which is "a good feeling about things." Rather it was akin to saying—go in complete wholeness. Jesus had made her whole. Physically she was made whole; spiritually she had her faith in the right place;

shalom

relationally she was given the opportunity to be made whole in community as well. This rightly and fully shows us a picture of peace—spiritual, physical, and relational wholeness.

Meanwhile, during Jesus' complete healing of the woman, the desperate father waited as his child died. He received the horrible news and was encouraged by the messenger (who believed Jesus was powerless in this situation) to leave Jesus alone. Yet, Jesus' response to the father engendered hope that all was not lost. Jesus told him not to fear the news and to believe that Jesus could still restore his daughter to life. He called him away from fear and to trust, and it rattled the father to the core of his being. How could he not fear the worst-case scenario news he was given? The news of his daughter's death had spread to the community, as mourners were already present outside of the family home. Subsequently, Jesus instructed the mourners to cease. Like the messenger, the mourners did not believe Jesus and laughed at Him. Jesus approached the deceased daughter, instructed her to rise, and by the power of His word she stood. Jesus, now concerned with the daughter's physical well being, instructed the awestruck parents to give her something to eat.

HEADS UP

Jesus' interaction with "Legion" shows the stark reality of the evil spiritual forces that were against Jesus and His followers. While we are not encouraged to pursue dark forces, we are called to be light in dark places; as a result, the darkness will not like it. The proper Christian position toward the demonic is not to be ignorant of their influence and presence, nor is it to get caught up in an unhealthy fascination with them (see Acts 19:13-16). The wonderful reality for Christians is that we are in union with Christ and thus have His power to overcome any attacks from the evil one. However, as Paul reminded the Ephesian Christians, our position in Christ does not reduce us to pure passivity. Rather we are to "put on the whole armor of God, that you may be able to stand against the schemes of the Devil. For we do not wrestle against flesh and blood, but against the rulers, against the authorities, against the cosmic powers over this present darkness, against the spiritual forces of evil in the heavenly places" (Eph. 6:11-12).

WARM-UP (10:00)

Have you ever felt totally powerless at an important point in your life? If so, what was it like? How did you deal with it?

SHOW SESSION 5 VIDEO: JESUS AND THE POWER OF GOD (10:00)

In this video, Dr. Carson points out that no life is so broken, no person so enslaved, and no sin so powerful that the power of Jesus cannot provide release. Each of these people had a very different situation. As a group, discuss how the power of God changed their lives.

GROUP DISCUSSION (20:00)

Why do you suppose the crowds reacted to Jesus in such a manner after He healed the demoniac? Have you ever felt afraid at the powerfulness of God's power? Explain why.

Why might the woman have wanted her healing to be in private? Have you ever wanted God's power to change something in your life so badly, but felt hesitant to ask Him for it, or even hesitant to ask others to pray with you for it? Why?

In the healing of the demoniac and the hemorrhaging women, we see Jesus heal them not simply of their ailments, but also of their social isolation. For Jesus, community reintegration is an important part of the salvation experience. Why do you think community is so important to Jesus?

Have you ever felt utterly out of control of a circumstance in your life? It's unsettling, yet as we see in these stories, being out of control led to healing and wholeness. With that in mind, how will your attitude toward bigger-than-you circumstances change?

In each of these three cases Jesus displays absolute power over these forces: demons, illness, and death. What seemingly unconquerable forces in your life do you want to hand over to Jesus to heal?

WRAP (10:00)

- Jesus had the power of God and was able to cast out demons, heal the sick, and bring the dead back to life.

- Jesus' ministry and power was not exclusive. It was open to anyone who came to Him in need and in faith.

- Faith in Jesus is not based on sentimental well-wishing. Faith in Jesus should be based on who He is and His proven power.

Close in prayer by asking God to bless each group member over the course of the week. Make time for the Take Home assignment below to enrich your experience with the Gospel of Luke.

TAKE HOME

Spend time this week reading and meditating on the following Scriptures: 2 Timothy 1:6-12, Romans 1:16-17, and Colossians 1:11-12. Based on these verses, in what ways can God's power work in the life someone who is connected with Jesus?

NOTES

JESUS AND THE MISSION OF GOD

SESSION 6

As we have seen so far, Jesus spent most of His ministry traveling in and around Galilee preaching the kingdom of God and showing the power of God's Word. After His remarkable resurrection of Jarius' daughter, Jesus' following swelled numerically and in zeal. Jesus sent the Twelve to heal and preach as well, and they accomplished their mission with astonishing success. As Luke summarized, the disciples "went through the villages, preaching the gospel and healing everywhere" (Luke 9:6). Following the widespread preaching and healing in the region by Jesus and His disciples, three of Jesus' disciples witnessed His transfiguration on the Mount of Olives in which His glory and divinity were showcased on earth as in heaven. On that mountain Jesus showed His divinity and also talked with saints of Israel's past, Moses and Elijah, about His upcoming journey to Jerusalem and all that was going to be accomplished there.

Yet, despite Jesus' proven power to heal and preach, the revelation of His divinity, and Peter's bold confession that Jesus was the Christ (Luke 9:20), the disciples remained unprepared for the necessary direction of Jesus' mission. Jesus turned from cheering crowds to humble obedience as He began a long and winding journey to Jerusalem. Following Jesus shifted from simply an opportunity for physical, earthly healing to a call to "take up one's own cross" and follow Jesus down a road riddled with heartache, rejection, and pain. Jesus further intensified and elaborated on the totality of His mission that would culminate with embracing His cross. None of Jesus' followers anticipated rejection and His death on a cross, but were preparing instead for a triumphal overthrow of Jerusalem. Ultimately, however, Jesus received the glory and exaltation of heaven and earth amidst a flurry of confusion and misplaced expectations.

51 When the days drew near for him to be taken up, he set his face to go to Jerusalem. 52 And he sent messengers ahead of him, who went and entered a village of the Samaritans, to make preparations for him. 53 But the people did not receive him, because his face was set toward Jerusalem. 54 And when his disciples James and John saw it, they said, "Lord, do you want us to tell fire to come down from heaven and consume them?" 55 But he turned and rebuked them. 56 And they went on to another village.

57 As they were going along the road, someone said to him, "I will follow you wherever you go." 58 And Jesus said to him, "Foxes have holes, and birds of the air have nests, but the Son of Man has nowhere to lay his head." 59 To another he said, "Follow me." But he said, "Lord, let me first go and bury my father." 60 And Jesus said to him, "Leave the dead to bury their own dead. But as for you, go and proclaim the kingdom of God." 61 Yet another said, "I will follow you, Lord, but let me first say farewell to those at my home." 62 Jesus said to him, "No one who puts his hand to the plow and looks back is fit for the kingdom of God."

COMMENTARY

Early in Luke's narrative, we observed Jesus as an eight-day-old infant in Jerusalem as He was presented in the temple. It was prophesied that in Jerusalem Jesus would bring salvation to Jews and Gentiles as the "light of revelation" to them. Another prophecy identified Jesus as the "appointed" one who would be opposed. Jesus would simultaneously bring salvation and be rejected. Luke 9 refocuses and clarifies earlier prophesies of the Jewish infant as Jesus set His face to return to Jerusalem. To this point in Jesus' ministry, He has concentrated His efforts on preaching the kingdom of God and demonstrating the power of God. Now the narrative shifts from Jesus' teaching and healing ministry (although these will still happen occasionally) to His journey to Jerusalem to demonstrate how one would be able to enter into this Kingdom. As alluded to in earlier prophesies and confirmed by Jesus' obedient action, entry into this Kingdom could only happen through the sacrifice of the King.

Jesus was going to Jerusalem to be rejected and killed. Indeed, He is even rejected by those whom His upcoming action would liberate spiritually. In the narrative, the Samaritans were specifically mentioned as "rejecting" Jesus. This development provides an ironic twist in the story as Jesus' focus on Jerusalem would provide the launching point that would make salvation for the Samaritans possible in the first place (Acts 1:8). Jesus demonstrated His love for the Samaritans during His journey (Luke 13), but that love would ultimately be demonstrated by His focus on the cross He would bear. The Samaritans desired for Him to continue His healing and teaching ministry in their region as He did in Galilee. However, their ultimate need would only be met when Jesus was allowed to complete His journey to Jerusalem. Even those closest to Jesus, His disciples, didn't fully understand His purposes in Jerusalem. He was not going to unleash wrath on sinners—as they wished to do to the Samaritans—but rather He was going to be a recipient of wrath on behalf of all sinners. In His infancy, Jesus' parents offered sacrifices for Him in Jerusalem, yet the purpose of His life was now to be the Lamb who would be the final sacrifice for all (see Luke 22:7-19). To complete His ministry and ultimately liberate the Jews, as well as Samaritans, Jesus had to set His face toward Jerusalem.

The phrase "set one's face" was an idiom, common in the Old Testament, indicating one's utter resolve to accomplish a mission. Jesus' mission would climax in Jerusalem on a cross. Luke highlights Jesus' shift of focus early in his narrative (fifteen chapters remain in his Gospel), and in so doing, he emphasizes the centrality of the cross and resurrection. While there are many important truths the disciples will learn on their journey with Jesus, it is Jesus' focus on the cross awaiting Him in Jerusalem that Luke emphasizes. The cross was and remains grossly misunderstood, and yet it was crucial for the disciples to fully understand Jesus and the totality of His purpose. The disciples probably understood some aspect of why Jerusalem was important to the ministry of Jesus, but they certainly did not understand the totality of the implications of the cross for their friend and the means by which He would be "taken up." His glory would be achieved via rejection and death, not by seizing political power. They were left to wrestle with the

Jesus "set His face" toward Jerusalem and the cross. That means He chose it, not for His own benefit, but for ours. Are you willing to set your face toward the mission God has for your life like Christ did? Why or why not?

Think about the safeguards you have in place to keep you from disaster. What things in your life are most difficult to let go of in order to contentedly trust in Jesus for all your needs? Explain why.

paradox and implications of following a Messiah who was heading to a cross to die.

In Luke 9:57-62, three potential followers learned the costs of following a soon-to-be crucified Messiah. First, a potential disciple declares to Jesus that he would follow Him anywhere. Yet Jesus' response directed the man to place his total security at Jesus' feet. Jesus further instructed that even animals who live day to day for survival have holes and nests to return to—but not so with following Jesus. To follow Jesus meant placing trust in nothing but Jesus Himself. By making this demand, Jesus separated Himself from the common rabbis of the day. Disciples of rabbis followed their teacher in order to learn and enhance their own lives. Here we see Jesus' call is a much more radical summons to mold one's own life in accordance with His will. Following Jesus was not simply a means by which one's own will was augmented by the insights of a guru, rather it was radically re-oriented to the Person of Jesus.

After the first interaction with a potential disciple, Jesus issued a call to an individual to abandon self-interests and follow Him. The man's response to Jesus' call seems reasonable and fits within the expected behavior of any good Jew. To bury one's father was a sacred responsibility and for Jesus to preempt it with His mission would cause any thoughtful Jew to pause and consider what Jesus was really asking. Jesus' call to this man was either the height of arrogance or Jesus' mission must be infused with the very authority of God. While Jesus' response to his request—let the dead bury the dead—seems harsh, it was not because Jesus wasn't compassionate toward those who lost loved ones (see John 11:28-37). Rather His eyes were set on defeating the root cause of all death and the Enemy that caused death itself. In order to accomplish this mission, He and those who desired to follow Him had to remain unencumbered by the trappings of tradition. Yahweh was again active and speaking into the human narrative through the Person and purpose of Jesus. Following Jesus allowed humanity to step into the divine narrative fulfilling the ultimate prophesy of the Old Testament, Jesus and a kingdom where death is fully and finally conquered.

The concept of humanity stepping into the divine narrative didn't die with Jesus on that cross or even in His resurrection. You are invited into God's narrative now. How does that make you feel? Does it feel like pressure or an honorable opportunity?

At the end of chapter 9, a third and final person approached Jesus and declared his desire to follow Him. We can presume that after eavesdropping on the two previous conversations with Jesus, he opted for a more nuanced approach. This man rightly understood that Jesus was not a common rabbi, but actively connected to the power of the living God. He also knew that God was present and active in the ministry of Jesus. Armed with an accurate awareness of Jesus, this man approached Jesus as a prophet of God. This savvy potential disciple requested to first say goodbye to his household as Elisha had also requested of the prophet Elijah in I Kings 19:19-20. Elijah granted Elisha's request and our seeker hoped for a similar response from Jesus. So, it was shocking to this individual that Jesus didn't follow the precedent and exhorted, "No one who puts his hand to the plow and looks back is fit for the kingdom of God" (Luke 9:52). By offering a rebuke instead of following Old Testament precedent, Jesus drew a stark distinction between Himself and all previous prophets. He was not simply a prophet in a line of prophets. Indeed, His purpose and ministry were unprecedented. Jesus' final interaction rightly reorients the reader to God's work and intervention into the human story as every prophet of old had foretold.

HEADS UP!

There remains a difficult aspect to the ministry of Jesus that His followers could never fully absorb. Sometimes Jesus would stop in a village and heal the sick but other times He would proceed through a village without pausing to heal anyone. As the Samaritans discovered, His purpose in their town was not to heal anyone immediately. There existed no pattern that Jesus was obliged to follow. Rather, Jesus demonstrated what it meant to follow the leading of the Spirit and what it means to be committed to one's ultimate calling and purpose. Sometimes this means enduring difficulty in the short term in order to achieve a larger and more impactful mission in the long term. The difficulty in following Jesus in paradoxical situations means that we are in a position of complete trust and must learn to depend on Him to make these difficult decisions.

WARM-UP (10:00)

Jesus' call to discipleship is contrary to the way many leaders recruit to their organization using bait and switch ploys that over-promise and under-deliver. In contrast, Jesus calls us to examine the cost before following Him, and as we read in this passage He does not sugarcoat those costs. Have you ever volunteered for something only to learn that the commitment was greater than what you had actually signed up for? If so, what was it like?

SHOW SESSION 6 VIDEO: JESUS AND THE MISSION OF GOD (10:00)

In this video, Dr. Carson points out the costs of following Jesus. In the three parables in Luke, Jesus lays out the costs of following Him. As a group, discuss these costs and what they mean for your life.

GROUP DISCUSSION (20:00)

"Jesus' glory would be achieved via rejection and death." How does that irony tie in with the outside-in theme highlighted in this study and in the Book of Luke? How does that theme apply to you and your role in God's mission?

"He and those who desired to follow Him had to remain unencumbered by the trappings of tradition." How have you seen tradition get in the way of God's bigger mission?

Those who desired to follow Jesus discovered that the costs were greater than they had expected. The same is true today. As a group, list some personal and general costs to following Jesus. Then ask yourself if it's worth it.

Jesus makes it crystal clear to His potential followers that He is unlike any other human ever born. How does His refusal to be compared affect your views of Him?

Jesus believed that our involvement in what He is doing is the most important and best thing we could possibly do. How could following Jesus be good for us when prioritizing our entire lives around Him demands painful sacrifice?

WRAP (10:00)

- Jesus did not come to unleash wrath on sinners, but rather to be the recipient of wrath on behalf of all sinners.

- Following Jesus means to "take up one's cross" and trust in nothing but Jesus Himself.

- Jesus was not simply another prophet in a long line of prophets. His ministry and purpose was unprecedented.

Close in prayer by asking God to bless each group member over the course of the week. Make time for the Take Home assignment below to enrich your experience with the Gospel of Luke.

TAKE HOME

Your assignment this week is to make a list of everything in your life that is important to you (family, friends, job, etc…). After completing the list (limit to 10 things), write Jesus' name on the top. What would it look like for you to really give these things over to Jesus? Which are the most difficult ones to prioritize?

NOTES

JESUS AND THE
COMPASSION
OF GOD

One of the key characteristics of God and His people is that they are compassionate. As the prophet Isaiah wrote, "Sing for joy, O heavens, and exult, O earth; break forth, O mountains, into singing! For the LORD has comforted his people and will have compassion on his afflicted" (Isa.49:13). To have compassion is to be moved to your core (literally it means to feel your insides/ guts churn!) for the sake of someone else. It is a concern for the "other" and their benefit that has set apart God's people for ages and in this passage we see that it too is the key feature of the ministry of Jesus.

After Jesus set His face to go to Jerusalem, He sent seventy-two followers ahead to the towns on His itinerary. The disciples had enormous success in these towns, as they later reported to Him, "Lord, even the demons are subject to us in your name!" Jesus was so delighted at the report that He prayed to the Father, "I thank you, Father, Lord of heaven and earth, that you have hidden these things from the wise and understanding and revealed them to little children; yes, Father, for such was your gracious will" (Luke 10:21). In the after glow of His success, an expert on the Jewish law emerged from the crowd. This lawyer with his religious question was motivated by a desire to frame Jesus' response in direct comparison to his highly educated religious knowledge. The response to his question would certainly affect Jesus and His credibility with the crowd, but would also demonstrate to the lawyer where Jesus "compared" to his own self-perceived legal expertise. Confounded by Jesus' response to the question, the lawyer left perplexed and more confused about the Jewish law. The lawyer had intended to test the knowledge of this itinerant teacher, but instead had his own religious foundations questioned. Jesus showed this teacher that being a neighbor means to show compassion to anyone who is in need.

25 And behold, a lawyer stood up to put him to the test, saying, "Teacher, what shall I do to inherit eternal life?" 26 He said to him, "What is written in the Law? How do you read it?" 27 And he answered, "You shall love the Lord your God with all your heart and with all your soul and with all your strength and with all your mind, and your neighbor as yourself." 28 And he said to him, "You have answered correctly; do this, and you will live."

29 But he, desiring to justify himself, said to Jesus, "And who is my neighbor?" 30 Jesus replied, "A man was going down from Jerusalem to Jericho, and he fell among robbers, who stripped him and beat him and departed, leaving him half dead. 31 Now by chance a priest was going down that road, and when he saw him he passed by on the other side. 32 So likewise a Levite, when he came to the place and saw him, passed by on the other side. 33 But a Samaritan, as he journeyed, came to where he was, and when he saw him, he had compassion. 34 He went to him and bound up his wounds, pouring on oil and wine. Then he set him on his own animal and brought him to an inn and took care of him. 35 And the next day he took out two denarii and gave them to the innkeeper, saying, 'Take care of him, and whatever more you spend, I will repay you when I come back.' 36 Which of these three, do you think, proved to be a neighbor to the man who fell among the robbers?" 37 He said, "The one who showed him mercy." And Jesus said to him, "You go, and do likewise."

COMMENTARY

After Jesus' disciples experienced one of their most successful moments recorded in Luke's Gospel, a lawyer emerged from the background to ask Jesus a question. By the tone of his question we understand him to be an onlooker to the ministry of Jesus—by no means is he a convinced follower. Jesus commonly allowed people who did not believe Him to follow Him from a distance and allowed them to occasionally ask questions. Here the lawyer posed an important question. He wasn't simply questioning Jesus about eternal life from sincere seeking, but from a desire to test Jesus. The lawyer stood while talking to Jesus which was a sign of respect juxtaposed against his true motive which was to not only to question Jesus' teaching, but to force Jesus to publicly align with himself. Jesus, however, knew the attitude of his heart and returned his question with a question. Jesus asked the lawyer, "What does the law say?" Jesus was not asking him to simply quote a scriptural reference, but rather He wanted to know how he understood what was written in Scripture. Jesus presented the lawyer with an opportunity to explain his understanding of the law. The lawyer's response was impressive and mimicked precisely how Jesus Himself had answered the same question earlier in His ministry. Yet, this lawyer was not satisfied with Jesus' answer and attempted to justify himself. His true motives were thus exposed, as he desired a rhetorical victory against Jesus, not simply a reached consensus. By asking, "who is my neighbor?" the lawyer opened up a teaching that he, and even Jesus' own disciples, were unprepared to understand.

By posing this question, he was asking who his neighbor was in an attempt to identify who his neighbor was not. This was a necessary qualification if his affirmation of the command of God was true. That is, of course, he loved his neighbors as himself if his neighbors were defined in a particular way.

It is important to note that this lawyer was not a straw man, but a real person with real questions. He had mixed motives as someone who had been watching Jesus from afar and observing the success of His followers. But, as Luke narrates, his motives in talking to Jesus were complicated. On the one hand, he called Jesus "teacher" and showed Him appropriate respect. On the other hand, his question to Jesus was not an honest inquiry, but asked in order to put Jesus to the test. While his question about eternal life showed that he was following Jesus' ministry closely, his desire to justify himself showed that he didn't actually understand the call and purpose of Jesus.

> Notice how the lawyer was trying to get out of the difficult task of loving others by asking for a more specific definition of who his neighbors are. If you catch yourself justifying your way out of obeying God's Word by altering or nitpicking the details of the command, what might this mean to you?

In response to the lawyer's follow up question, Jesus told a story about a "certain man" who was robbed and beaten on the road to Jericho from Jerusalem. This path was famously treacherous and packed with many spots in which brigands could lie in wait for their victims. The fact that this man was not given an ethnicity but the generic designation "certain man" showed that the hearer was to place himself in the position of the "certain man." After he was robbed and beaten, two religious figures passed by—first, a priest and second, a Levite. Both passed on the other side of the road refusing to help. At this point Jesus introduced a Samaritan into the story and the Samaritan acted in a way expected of the priest and Levite—he helped the man in need. Indeed, he not only helped, but he helped in a manner that far exceeded the most basic expectations of kindness. He even placed himself at financial risk by assuring the innkeeper that he would continue to pay what was owed in caring for this sick stranger.

This story has many compelling aspects but the one that is profoundly obvious is that the hero in the story was the Samaritan. The multi-faceted Jewish hatred of the Samaritans was well-known. For hundreds of years foreign enemies of Israel had found refuge in Samaria. Indeed, there was a military outpost for the Greeks in Samaria for years. When the Romans defeated the Greeks, they found a welcoming community to allow them to establish a military presence as well. In Jesus' day Samaria was decidedly pro-Roman. Religiously, they were the offspring of Jews who intermarried with pagans. The result was that they had a deeply misconstrued understanding of Judaism, rejected most of the Hebrew Scriptures (except the first 5 books), and refused to believe that Jerusalem was a proper place to worship. As seen in Luke 9, some of Jesus' disciples would have eagerly spearheaded the sudden and total destruction of Samaria. Samaritans were a godless and despicable people in the eyes of Israel and certainly not to be the featured hero in a tale told by a Jewish teacher. Jesus' story shattered real and perceived barriers of the day and provided a welcoming outstretched hand to the outcasts of society.

One of the striking features of Jesus' story is not that the Samaritan was the example to follow—"go and do likewise"—but the premise of the question "who is my neighbor?" is obliterated. As the Samaritan demonstrated, he did not ask the ethnicity, pedigree, nationality, or social status of the neighbor in need before intervening. Instead, the issue was not, "who is one's neighbor," but whether or not someone decides *to be* a neighbor.

Another important issue confronted in the passage—which may have been the more challenging one to Jesus' audience—is that *anyone* can be a neighbor. The Old Testament definition of neighbor was understood to be someone who was in the covenant of God, either an Israelite or a foreigner welcomed into the community of Israel. Here Jesus is making an obvious divergence from the previous definition of the family of God and neighbor. The definition of neighbor expanded and was identified by different criteria than had been used before. The lawyer, as well as Jesus' disciples, would be confused to learn that a Samaritan was the one in Jesus' story who embodied the Jewish law. How could that be? Yet, Jesus' point was that this Samaritan indeed fulfilled the law of loving one's neighbor, and it rightly challenged the lawyer's categories and understanding. Jesus' follow-up question forced the lawyer to admit that this hated outsider was indeed the picture of obedience to the law.

The story then shifted from the lawyer's actions toward other people to how he received the actions of others. A third issue in the story was whether or not the lawyer would become humble enough to be "neighbored" by someone who was not from his tribe. Would he be able to receive help from someone who he believed was not worthy of acknowledgment and had nothing to contribute?

This beautiful narrative ushered in a new universal scope for salvation. Anyone, including the outcasts, marginalized, and shunned of society, could now experience Jesus' salvation and transformation. This Samaritan had compassion on a Jew. The compassion of the Samaritan was an echo of the compassion that Jesus Himself had for the widow who lost her son. It was a compassion that came from God. For all of Jesus' ancient listeners, this very image would be an oxymoron. Their prejudice was so ingrained that they likely vehemently questioned Jesus' teaching when He described it. Indeed, when Jesus asked the lawyer who his neighbor was, the lawyer couldn't verbally utter the word Samaritan, and instead responded with "the one that showed mercy."

Just as Jesus challenged His followers to re-think who their neighbors were, His disciples today are summoned to do the same. Jesus' teaching calls everyone who claims His name to examine their networks and assess if there are people in their lives that they have deemed "off limits" to God's compassion. Jesus' teaching on the Samaritan ought to provoke His disciples to re-imagine their social world in a way in which compassion is shown to all in need.

How difficult will it be to make your standard of love and being a neighbor match Jesus' standard? Who in your life do you need to start with?

HEADS UP!

One of the fundamentals of the gospel is that there is nothing anyone can do to achieve eternal life. Eternal life is a gift freely given by God as an act of grace. It is to be received by faith and cannot be earned by works. If that is the case, why then did Jesus answer the lawyer's question about eternal life by asking him a question in return? Why not simply tell him the real answer and gain a convert in the process? The reason is that the lawyer was not ready for the answer. Jesus was always careful to reveal barriers that obstructed one's understanding of His good news. And for this lawyer, until he understood that he was a lawbreaker, he would see no need for the good news Jesus brought.

WARM-UP (10:00)

Have you even known someone from afar and had opinions formed about that person, only to have those opinions changed when you actually got to know them? If so, what was that process like?

WATCH SESSION 7 VIDEO: JESUS AND THE COMPASSION OF GOD (10:00)

In this video, Dr. Carson tells the story of the Good Samaritan and explains that "Jesus is full of compassion toward the broken." When Jesus tells the lawyer, "Go and do likewise," Dr. Carson reminds us that we are not saved because of our obedience. Rather, obedience is a characteristic of those who have been saved by Christ. As a group, discuss ways that God has shown you compassion, and ways you can show compassion to others.

GROUP DISCUSSION (20:00)

Jesus is strong enough to handle our toughest questions and welcomes the opportunity to teach us His ways. But when do you think questioning might become sinful?

Why did the Jews hate the Samaritans? What would be the most shocking aspect of Jesus making a Samaritan an example to follow?

You may hate or avoid others in the name of protecting the honor of God's Word and the Person of Jesus. But based on the parable Jesus told, how does He feel about that?

Which aspect of the lawyer's understanding of the law had to be rethought if a Samaritan could embody the law itself?

_____

_____

_____

_____

The lawyer would probably have a hard time accepting the kindness from an enemy or someone he considered generally unworthy. Perhaps you do too. What would your salvation story be if Jesus abided by the lawyer's narrow standard of mercy rather than God's wide one?

_____

_____

_____

_____

What is the most difficult challenge for you in being a true neighbor?

_____

_____

_____

_____

WRAP (10:00)

- Jesus demonstrated the proper way to love one's neighbor.

- Anyone, including the outcasts, marginalized, and shunned of society, can experience Jesus' salvation and transformation. No one is "off limits."

- Eternal life is a gift freely given by God as an act of grace. There is nothing anyone can do to earn it.

Close in prayer by asking God to bless each group member over the course of the week. Make time for the Take Home assignment below to enrich your experience with the Gospel of Luke.

TAKE HOME

Honestly examine your own posture toward the different types of people in your life. Is there a person or group of people that you treat as if the gospel is not for them? Who is it? Why do you view them in this light? What can you do this week to change your posture toward them and demonstrate that change?

NOTES

JESUS AND THE GRACE OF GOD

As Jesus' long journey to Jerusalem continued, He still attracted crowds and was willing to enter into to the homes of both religious folk (see Luke 11:37-52) and irreligious folk (see Luke 15). Jesus' message however had such a sharp edge to it that many in the crowds were offended. As a lawyer told Jesus outright, "Teacher, in saying these things you insult us also" (11:45). Jesus however needed to explain to His curious onlookers the weight of the decision that was before them in following Him. Following Jesus was like entering the narrow door (13:22-30) and if anyone desired to follow Him he must first count the cost (14:25-33). Yet, whatever the cost was in following Jesus, it could never amount to the lasting treasure of eternal life (12:13-21).

In the text at hand, we see that many unlikely candidates had counted the costs and decided to follow after Jesus. These tax collectors and sinners drew near to Jesus and we see them celebrating with Jesus. What were they celebrating? Jesus' parables explain that He was celebrating the return of His long lost sheep. But would the religious folk join in on the party?

TEXT: LUKE 15

Now the tax collectors and sinners were all drawing near to hear him. ² And the Pharisees and the scribes grumbled, saying, "This man receives sinners and eats with them."

³ So he told them this parable: ⁴ "What man of you, having a hundred sheep, if he has lost one of them, does not leave the ninety-nine in the open country, and go after the one that is lost, until he finds it? ⁵ And when he has found it, he lays it on his shoulders, rejoicing. ⁶ And when he comes home, he calls together his friends and his neighbors, saying to them, 'Rejoice with me, for I have found my sheep that was lost.' ⁷ Just so, I tell you, there will be more joy in heaven over one sinner who repents than over ninety-nine righteous persons who need no repentance.

⁸ "Or what woman, having ten silver coins, if she loses one coin, does not light a lamp and sweep the house and seek diligently until she finds it? ⁹ And when she has found it, she calls together her friends and neighbors, saying, 'Rejoice with me, for I have found the coin that I had lost.' ¹⁰ Just so, I tell you, there is joy before the angels of God over one sinner who repents."

¹¹ And he said, "There was a man who had two sons. ¹² And the younger of them said to his father, 'Father, give me the share of property that is coming to me.' And he divided his property between them. ¹³ Not many days later, the younger son gathered all he had and took a journey into a far country, and there he squandered his property in reckless living. ¹⁴ And when

he had spent everything, a severe famine arose in that country, and he began to be in need. [15] So he went and hired himself out to one of the citizens of that country, who sent him into his fields to feed pigs. [16] And he was longing to be fed with the pods that the pigs ate, and no one gave him anything.

[17] "But when he came to himself, he said, 'How many of my father's hired servants have more than enough bread, but I perish here with hunger! [18] I will arise and go to my father, and I will say to him, "Father, I have sinned against heaven and before you. [19] I am no longer worthy to be called your son. Treat me as one of your hired servants."' [20] And he arose and came to his father. But while he was still a long way off, his father saw him and felt compassion, and ran and embraced him and kissed him. [21] And the son said to him, 'Father, I have sinned against heaven and before you. I am no longer worthy to be called your son.' [22] But the father said to his servants, 'Bring quickly the best robe, and put it on him, and put a ring on his hand, and shoes on his feet. [23] And bring the fattened calf and kill it, and let us eat and celebrate. [24] For this my son was dead, and is alive again; he was lost, and is found.' And they began to celebrate.

[25] "Now his older son was in the field, and as he came and drew near to the house, he heard music and dancing. [26] And he called one of the servants and asked what these things meant. [27] And he said to him, 'Your brother has come, and your father has killed the fattened calf, because he has received him back safe and sound.' [28] But he was angry and refused to go

Are you guilty of holding people to a different standard than Jesus does? If so, how do you justify it? How have you seen this type of attitude affect those who are lost?

in. His father came out and entreated him, ²⁹ but he answered his father, 'Look, these many years I have served you, and I never disobeyed your command, yet you never gave me a young goat, that I might celebrate with my friends. ³⁰ But when this son of yours came, who has devoured your property with prostitutes, you killed the fattened calf for him!' ³¹ And he said to him, 'Son, you are always with me, and all that is mine is yours. ³² It was fitting to celebrate and be glad, for this your brother was dead, and is alive; he was lost, and is found.'"

COMMENTARY

This chapter begins with sinners and tax-collectors drawing near to Jesus. Sinners were individuals who found themselves on the outside of the community because of their irreligious lifestyles. Tax collectors were equally despised by the community because they worked for the Romans in taxing their fellow Jews. Yet, both of these groups were drawing near to Jesus. There was attractiveness to Jesus' message and Person that made these outcasts believe He would welcome them. Yet their coming to Jesus was not the result of some kind of cheap grace. Based on Jesus' teaching on counting the cost, these sinners were coming to Jesus as repentant sinners. The fact that Jesus welcomed them without a prolonged period of penance is what got Him crossways with the Pharisees and scribes.

The religious authorities did not like Jesus' pattern of welcoming these types of people (5:27-32; 7:29-30). Their grumbling at Jesus' apparently reckless acceptance would gain steam as later the whole community would join in the grumbling (19:7). Not only did Jesus welcome them, but He also ate with them. In that culture, to eat with someone who was unclean, as sinners were deemed to be, was to become unclean as well. Yet, as illustrated in Jesus' stories, instead of Him becoming unclean, He declared that these sinners were in fact repentant and restored to their spiritual family.

In response to the criticism, Jesus told three stories that all shared a similar theme: when something valuable is returned home, that is cause to celebrate. The first story was about a shepherd who left his 99 sheep in order to find the one that had strayed. After finding the sheep, the man hoisted it on his shoulders and returned home. He then called his friends over for a party to celebrate. This story highlights the proactive seeking of the lost that was so prominent in Jesus' ministry. He was not just accepting those who came to Him, but He was actively seeking those who had left the fold. Of course, to the 99, His leaving them may have seemed reckless, but His actions underscored the deep love He had for each sheep.

The second story was of a woman who had lost a valuable coin and after searching, she at last found it. She too called her friends together to rejoice with her finding the coin. In both instances, Jesus said that in heaven, the angels rejoice when just one sinner repents. That Jesus described these individuals as repentant is very important because this denotes their attitude toward their relationship with Jesus. Unlike the lawyer in our previous session, these sinners came to Jesus not as curious on-lookers, but as contrite sinners seeking forgiveness. Jesus celebrating with them indicated that their repentance was accepted and their membership among God's people had been completed.

In each of the first two stories Jesus brought His listeners into the story by introducing it in a rhetorically inviting way. The first story starts with "which of you, if he had a hundred sheep…" and the second starts with "what woman with ten silver coins, if she loses one, does not…" What Jesus is doing with this rhetoric is showing a proper perspective of His actions so as to persuade this audience that He was, in fact, doing the right thing by spending time with these sinners. If individuals would celebrate the return of a sheep or of a coin, how much more ought they celebrate the return of a soul into God's family? Indeed, if heaven itself erupts with celebration upon the return of one sinner, shouldn't the scribes and Pharisees join with the angels in this celebration?

The last story Jesus told is similar to the first two with one significant difference. In this story, Jesus lets us in on the thought-process of the son as he engaged in a prolonged act of repentance. The story begins with a straightforward sentence: "a man had two sons." After that, we learn that the younger of the two sons insisted on receiving his inheritance from his father. To make such a request, in that culture, was like saying you wished your father to be dead. But, shockingly, the father granted the son's selfish request. After the son left his father's house, he quickly wasted his money and found himself in real trouble. He was out of money and found work feeding pigs, which as a Jew, was as low as one could get. Indeed, he was feeding pigs while he himself was starving.

In the midst of starvation, he decided to return home to his father. Yet, because of the offense he knew that his status as a son had been irreversibly revoked. He decided to ask his father if he could be a servant because that would at least provide food and shelter. He rehearsed his speech and started his journey home.

What does the parable of the lost sheep tell you about your worth to God? How does it impact the way you view those who are wandering from the faith?

At the end of his journey, he was finally within sight of his father. At this point in the narrative, the son was no longer the active agent in the story—the father was. The father ran to greet his son and immediately embraced him. The son began his lines that he had rehearsed earlier, but his father cut him off and didn't allow him to finish. The father immediately called to his servant and demanded proper clothes for his son who was no doubt in rags and barefooted. He also placed a ring on his finger as sign of full status as son and heir of the father. After this he called for a huge celebration because his son, who was lost, had now been found. Indeed, he was not just lost; his son was dead and had now been made alive.

In the final scene of this story the elder son took center stage. The dilemma he was faced with was whether or not he would receive his wayward younger brother. It was a bitter pill to swallow because his brother was the center of a celebration when he had wasted his father's money on sinful indulgences. The older son explained to his father that he had been slaving for his father for many years and that it didn't seem fair that his brother received all of this extravagant undeserved favor. The father retorted that everything he had belonged to the elder brother and that he too should join in the celebration of his younger brother who had come back from the dead. The scene ends with the elder brother left with a decision to make: would he join in the celebration of his younger brother's return or would he remain bitter that his father had accepted this sinner back into his house? It is an ironic scene because the elder brother saw himself as a slave (v. 29), just as the younger brother had planned on becoming. Yet the father received the prodigal as a son, and we are left to wonder if the elder son would receive the love of his father as well.

This last scene is a reminder that Jesus not only sought the outcast and the obvious sinner, but also reached out to the religious. Jesus wanted to be in fellowship with those who tried hard to obey, as well as those who had failed miserably.

Who in your world do you deem unworthy of your time? Your mercy? Your love? Following Jesus' example, how can you improve the way you interact with those specific people in times when they are trying to obey and in times when they are failing miserably?

HEADS UP

The story of the prodigal son provides a wonderful picture of divine and human agency at work in conversion. Jesus gives us insight into what the son was thinking when he decided to return to the father. Indeed, the moment of return was when the son "came to himself" which is akin to coming to one's senses. Yet his return was not an instant one, for what he wanted for himself (to be a servant) was much lower than what his father wished for him. When he arose and headed home we see the father come out to meet him. Even though the son expressed an active agency in returning to the father, the father's proclamation that the son who was dead is now alive is an act of absolute divine grace. It is important to point out this dynamic because when an individual comes to Jesus, there is a sense in which they themselves are doing the seeking, but after they come to Jesus, they can look back and see that it was Jesus who was actively seeking them and who brought them to life as a gift of grace.

WARM-UP (10:00)

Have you ever been forgiven of something that you have done? If so, what was it and how did it feel to be welcomed back into a relationship?

SHOW SESSION 8 VIDEO: JESUS AND THE GRACE OF GOD (10:00)

In this video, Dr. Carson summarizes the three parables in Luke 15. Each parable is about someone losing something special to them—a sheep, a coin, and a son. Jesus explains in each parable that when the lost are found, there is reason to celebrate. Out of sheer grace, God seeks out the hopeless, lost, and sick. As a group, discuss a time when Jesus actively sought after you. How did you respond?

GROUP DISCUSSION (20:00)

In this session, we get to talk about an attribute of Jesus that many people struggle to appreciate. How does Jesus' reckless acceptance of "undeserving" outsiders make you feel?

You've likely been around modern-day Pharisees whose intense quest for righteousness ends up creating bitterness, even stinginess in their hearts. How does knowing their initial pursuit was good and honorable change the way you think about and deal with them?

_____

_____

_____

Have you ever given someone or been given a hard time following a return to Jesus? What do you wish you could change about the experience?

_____

_____

_____

In the parable of the prodigal son, the father represents God. As a group, list the qualities of God exhibited through the father. What, if anything, surprises you about Him?

_____

_____

_____

Why was it so hard for the older brother to accept the return of his younger brother and his father's behavior toward him? What do you think is the root of those negative feelings when someone sees another return to God?

_____

_____

_____

Who do you identify with most, the prodigal son or the elder brother? Talk about how that plays itself out in your relationship with other people and with God.

WRAP (10:00)

- Jesus accepts sinners and restores them to their spiritual families.

- Jesus does not just seek out the outcast and obvious sinner, but also the religious, the ones who try hard to obey.

- Jesus is actively seeking the lost and showing them grace.

Close in prayer by asking God to bless each group member over the course of the week. Make time for the Take Home assignment below to enrich your experience with the Gospel of Luke.

TAKE HOME

We live in a performance based civilization to which Jesus' display of grace radically stands in opposition. Your assignment this week is to study Ephesians 2:1-10. How does this passage describe those who don't know Jesus? What is it that makes them come to life? Discuss your answers with your group in next week's meeting.

NOTES

JESUS AND THE
SALVATION
OF GOD

After the story of the prodigal son, Jesus continued to baffle the Pharisees with His teaching on finances (see Luke 16:1-14) and eternity (vv. 19-31). He pointed out that one often gets in the way of the other. Jesus then encountered a young ruler who desired to know about the eternal life that Jesus had to offer. The barrier between this man and eternal life however was his love for money. Jesus identified this barrier very quickly and the man left very sad, unwilling to overcome it. This man wanted to fit Jesus into his life when following Jesus meant reordering his life around Jesus. He had too much to lose—yet by this thinking, he lost everything (see Luke12:16-21).

Now nearing Jerusalem, Jesus traveled through Jericho where He encountered another rich man. This one was an infamous, diminutive tax collector named Zacchaeus. While the rich man in chapter 18 was considered righteous, this tax collector in Jericho was deemed a sinner. However, the twist to these two stories is that only one of these rich men would experience salvation. After the righteous ruler went away sad, Jesus' disciples asked out loud, "Who then could be saved?" The surprising answer to this question will come in the house of someone who was clearly unrighteous. Zacchaeus desired to see Jesus while remaining unnoticed on the outside, but it was Jesus who pursued this sinner, summoning him to come down from the tree. Jesus' closing statement punctuated His action toward this sinner: "For the Son of Man came to seek and to save the lost" (19:10).

TEXT: LUKE 19:1-10

¹ He entered Jericho and was passing through. ² And behold, there was a man named Zacchaeus. He was a chief tax collector and was rich. ³ And he was seeking to see who Jesus was, but on account of the crowd he could not, because he was small in stature. ⁴ So he ran on ahead and climbed up into a sycamore tree to see him, for he was about to pass that way. ⁵ And when Jesus came to the place, he looked up and said to him, "Zacchaeus, hurry and come down, for I must stay at your house today." ⁶ So he hurried and came down and received him joyfully. ⁷ And when they saw it, they all grumbled, "He has gone in to be the guest of a man who is a sinner." ⁸ And Zacchaeus stood and said to the Lord, "Behold, Lord, the half of my goods I give to the poor. And if I have defrauded anyone of anything, I restore it fourfold." ⁹ And Jesus said to him, "Today salvation has come to this house, since he also is a son of Abraham. ¹⁰ For the Son of Man came to seek and to save the lost."

COMMENTARY

One of the many adjustments I needed to make when I got married was learning to give my wife a call before coming home with an unexpected guest. To have a stranger over unexpectedly put her in a vulnerable situation. A sudden drop-in exposed us to possible silent judgments such as people thinking, "Look how dirty their house is!" or to face unmet expectations: "I used to think they had their act together, but it sure doesn't look like it." To expose our house to someone was to expose our lives—both the good and the bad. And our anxiety of having our lives open to others was either rewarded or regretted based on the attitude of the one we invited in. In this story we will see Jesus invite Himself into an unlikely person's house, and into the scandal that took place once He entered.

The story of Zacchaeus is one of the most well-known stories in the Bible. The image of a short tax collector climbing a sycamore tree to catch a glimpse of Jesus has long captured the imagination of readers both young and old. Children read this story and identify with being crowded out, not able to see over the heads of those who are taller. Growing Christians read this and identify with the sometimes sudden entrance of Jesus into their lives, having little time to "clean up" before He makes Himself at home.

In order to understand this story better, we need to get to know Zacchaeus. Luke points out that Zacchaeus was not just a tax collector, but the chief tax collector in Jericho. This city, residing just outside of Jerusalem, was a major import/export center. So, as chief tax collector in that city, he found himself to be in an extremely profitable situation. In that region, taxes were not fixed locally, so tax collectors could adjust them as much as they desired. In case there was any doubt, Luke adds that Zacchaeus was "rich." Tax collectors in this region were Jews working for the oppressors of Jews, so we begin to understand how they were perceived. It is no wonder tax collectors were hated and found themselves on the outside of the community, cast off as sinners. Hence, to be in Zacchaeus' position he had to have made a decision that being wealthy was more important to him than being accepted. He loved money more than people. Yet despite all of his wealth, there was still something missing. Furthermore, he believed Jesus could give insight into what that missing piece was. Here we learn that Zacchaeus was not going to be like the rich ruler in chapter 18. Zacchaeus was willing to be undignified in order to get a peek at Jesus by climbing a tree like a child.

So there was Zacchaeus, up in a tree, hoping to catch a glimpse of this controversial rabbi. What Zacchaeus already knew of Jesus is uncertain. All we know is that he wanted to see Him and creatively maneuvered past his own physical barriers in order to do just that. What happened next was likely just as shocking to him as it was to all of the onlookers. Jesus stopped near the tree, looked up directly at the tax collector and called him by name. Luke doesn't indicate how Jesus knew his name, but the fact that He stopped and instructed him to come down quickly indicated that Jesus had a plan for this sinner.

Zacchaeus responded to Jesus' shocking invitation joyfully and he welcomed Him into his house with no reservations. Zacchaeus demonstrated a changed heart by giving up the very thing he held onto the most. In Judaism, repentance was not just a declaration that one had repented, but there would also be a demonstration of repentance ("fruit of repentance"). After only one encounter with Jesus, the thing Zacchaeus once held

We read in God's Word that we are to love God first and love others second. What things in your life have a tendency to slip into that second-place slot where "people" should be?

Zacchaeus instantaneously and willingly let go of his most prized possession when he encountered Christ. When have you experienced a shift in your priorities because of Jesus? What prized possession lost its luster to you at that time? How do you keep that thing in its proper place?

Jesus continually surprised His audience by His actions, especially by the way He treated outsiders. Whether or not you realize it, you have an audience as well. What "Jesus thing" can you do to surprise them this week?

dear meant nothing to him. He gave half of his wealth to the poor—without Jesus even asking!—and then gave back four times what he swindled from others. This is the holistic nature of repentance. It is not just a personal, private religious experience, but one that has immediate implications in real life. Repentance to Jesus restores one's relationship with God, but also plants a desire to restore relationships with others.

Careful readers will observe a similarity between this story and the parable of the the prodigal son. The human-divine agency worked almost identically in these two stories. Luke notes that Zacchaeus was seeking out Jesus, yet it was Jesus who called him by name and took center stage in his life. For the prodigal, he decided to return home but the father saw him from far away and took over the narrative from that point on. For both Zacchaeus and the prodigal, their expectation of Jesus/father was far less than what Jesus/father had in store for them. Zacchaeus and the prodigal would have settled to be curious onlookers and slaves. But what Jesus and the forgiving father had in mind was full inclusion as sons in God's family.

This is how conversion often works. For the seeker, there is an honest quest to discover who God is and what He wants from him. Once that person "discovers" Jesus, then they can look back and realize that it was Jesus who discovered them—hiding in a tree— and called them by name and ushered them into God's family.

HEADS UP!

Understanding how salvation happens in the lives of individuals is a mysterious thing—yet it happens—and it happened to Zacchaeus in this story. Here we see that Jesus going to Zacchaeus' house was followed by a declaration by Jesus that salvation had come to his house. The point that Luke made by arranging his narrative this way was to highlight that wherever Jesus was, salvation was soon to follow. The experience of salvation, sometimes called conversion, is for some a particular moment in time—as it is here when Jesus declared that "today" salvation was in this house. Yet, for many others, conversion is a longer process in which they can look back and see that Jesus had transformed them over time, or that they can confess that they were trusting in Jesus, but can't recall the moment in time when that transition happened. The moment certainly occurred; they simply are not aware of the specific time or place. In Luke's second volume, Acts, we see that many people would turn to Jesus and experience conversion. Yet, they too would experience it in slightly different ways. The important thing is understanding who Jesus is, where He stands in your life, and whether or not you have yielded control of your life to Him. The question about how it is He saves us will be explored in next week's study.

WARM UP (10:00)

When you hear the word "salvation," what things come to mind? What do you see? Who do you think of?

SHOW SESSION 9 VIDEO: JESUS AND THE SALVATION OF GOD (10:00)

In this video, Dr. Carson discusses the story of Zacchaeus and how his life was transformed when Jesus came to his house. Zacchaeus gave up more than half of his wealth after meeting Jesus, because Jesus showed mercy on him. As a group, discuss the story of Zacchaeus and think of a time in your life when God showed mercy toward you when you least deserved it.

GROUP DISCUSSION (20:00)

If you have ever been called from a crowd unexpectedly by someone who was in the spotlight, describe how it felt to go suddenly from spectator to participant. In this story, Jesus made Zacchaeus a participant. How has Jesus made you a participant in His story?

When the crowd saw that Jesus went into Zacchaeus' house, it was not just the religious folks who grumbled, but the entire crowd. In their eyes, Jesus had gone too far in befriending this enemy of Israel. What kinds of people are you sometimes tempted to think should be off limits to Jesus' friendship? Who do you know who befriends those outsiders?

_____

_____

_____

_____

What was so surprising and frankly, frustrating, about Jesus' pursuit of a man like Zacchaeus? What does this demonstrate to us about Jesus and our view of salvation?

_____

_____

_____

_____

Zacchaeus didn't know a lot about Jesus, but he realized that day that what Jesus offered was better than money. Talk about the top things people cling to instead of opening their hands to what Jesus has. What is or was your "thing"?

_____

_____

_____

_____

We read, "repentance to Jesus restores one's relationship with God, but also plants a desire to restore relationships with others." Along those lines, then, do you believe a person can have a healthy relationship with God while their relationships with others remain in shambles?

If Jesus operated on an insiders-only basis, like the religious people wanted Him to, how would the world be different? How would the church be different? How would you?

WRAP (10:00)

- Repentance is not just a personal, private experience, but one that has immediate implications for others.

- Repentance and faith in Jesus restores one's relationship with God, but also plants a desire to restore relationships with others.

- Wherever Jesus is, salvation is soon to follow.

Close in prayer by asking God to bless each group member over the course of the week. Make time for the Take Home assignment below to enrich your experience with the Gospel of Luke.

TAKE HOME

Read Romans 10:1-10 this week. How does Paul say that one can experience salvation? How does what Paul writes here align with Zacchaeus' story?

NOTES

JESUS THE LAMB OF GOD

Last week we read about Zacchaeus' experience of salvation and that Jesus was the One who was able to bring it into reality for him. This week we will learn how Jesus was able to bring salvation. Salvation was not a glib proclamation nor was it a superficial experience, but it was achieved at a great cost. Salvation is a free gift for those who receive it, but, as we will see, it was very costly for Jesus.

In the beginning of Luke's Gospel we witnessed the infant Jesus in Jerusalem and He was the subject of several prophecies concerning His divine vocation. In chapter nine of the Gospel we saw Jesus' focus directed to this city as He began His long journey toward it. In chapter nineteen we see Jesus finally arrive in Jerusalem ready to fulfill His mission. Jesus' entry into the city was jubilant, but cries of praise quickly turned into cries of "crucify Him!"

Now that the hour had come for Jesus to experience unparalleled suffering, how would He respond to this final test? Now that Israel's Messiah had come to rescue her from her real oppressors, how would she respond to this definitive moment of God's "visitation"? In the narrative of Jesus' betrayal and crucifixion, God's ancient plan of salvation emerged from a flurry of injustice directed at His Son. This "hour of darkness" was at the very same time the greatest expression of God's love for the world.

[1] Now the Feast of Unleavened Bread drew near, which is called the Passover. [2] And the chief priests and the scribes were seeking how to put him to death, for they feared the people.

[3] Then Satan entered into Judas called Iscariot, who was of the number of the twelve. [4] He went away and conferred with the chief priests and officers how he might betray him to them. [5] And they were glad, and agreed to give him money. [6] So he consented and sought an opportunity to betray him to them in the absence of a crowd.

[7] Then came the day of Unleavened Bread, on which the Passover lamb had to be sacrificed. [8] So Jesus sent Peter and John, saying, "Go and prepare the Passover for us, that we may eat it." [9] They said to him, "Where will you have us prepare it?" [10] He said to them, "Behold, when you have entered the city, a man carrying a jar of water will meet you. Follow him into the house that he enters [11] and tell the master of the house, 'The Teacher says to you, Where is the guest room, where I may eat the Passover with my disciples?' [12] And he will show you a large upper room furnished; prepare it there." [13] And they went and found it just as he had told them, and they prepared the Passover.

[14] And when the hour came, he reclined at table, and the apostles with him. [15] And he said to them, "I have earnestly desired to eat this Passover with you before I suffer. [16] For I tell you I will not eat it until it is fulfilled in the kingdom of God." [17] And he took a cup, and when

he had given thanks he said, "Take this, and divide it among yourselves. ¹⁸ For I tell you that from now on I will not drink of the fruit of the vine until the kingdom of God comes." ¹⁹ And he took bread, and when he had given thanks, he broke it and gave it to them, saying, "This is my body, which is given for you. Do this in remembrance of me." ²⁰ And likewise the cup after they had eaten, saying, "This cup that is poured out for you is the new covenant in my blood. ²¹ But behold, the hand of him who betrays me is with me on the table. ²² For the Son of Man goes as it has been determined, but woe to that man by whom he is betrayed!" ²³ And they began to question one another, which of them it could be who was going to do this.

²⁴ A dispute also arose among them, as to which of them was to be regarded as the greatest. ²⁵ And he said to them, "The kings of the Gentiles exercise lordship over them, and those in authority over them are called benefactors. ²⁶ But not so with you. Rather, let the greatest among you become as the youngest, and the leader as one who serves. ²⁷ For who is the greater, one who reclines at table or one who serves? Is it not the one who reclines at table? But I am among you as the one who serves.

²⁸ "You are those who have stayed with me in my trials, ²⁹ and I assign to you, as my Father assigned to me, a kingdom, ³⁰ that you may eat and drink at my table in my kingdom and sit on thrones judging the twelve tribes of Israel.

³¹ "Simon, Simon, behold, Satan demanded to have you, that he might sift you like wheat, ³² but I have

prayed for you that your faith may not fail. And when you have turned again, strengthen your brothers."
[33] Peter said to him, "Lord, I am ready to go with you both to prison and to death." [34] Jesus said, "I tell you, Peter, the rooster will not crow this day, until you deny three times that you know me."

[35] And he said to them, "When I sent you out with no moneybag or knapsack or sandals, did you lack anything?" They said, "Nothing." [36] He said to them, "But now let the one who has a moneybag take it, and likewise a knapsack. And let the one who has no sword sell his cloak and buy one. [37] For I tell you that this Scripture must be fulfilled in me: 'And he was numbered with the transgressors.' For what is written about me has its fulfillment." [38] And they said, "Look, Lord, here are two swords." And he said to them, "It is enough."

[39] And he came out and went, as was his custom, to the Mount of Olives, and the disciples followed him. [40] And when he came to the place, he said to them, "Pray that you may not enter into temptation." [41] And he withdrew from them about a stone's throw, and knelt down and prayed, [42] saying, "Father, if you are willing, remove this cup from me. Nevertheless, not my will, but yours, be done." [43] And there appeared to him an angel from heaven, strengthening him. [44] And being in an agony he prayed more earnestly; and his sweat became like great drops of blood falling down to the ground. [45] And when he rose from prayer, he came to the disciples and found them sleeping for sorrow, [46] and he said to them, "Why are you sleeping? Rise and pray that you may not enter into temptation."

47 While he was still speaking, there came a crowd, and the man called Judas, one of the twelve, was leading them. He drew near to Jesus to kiss him, 48 but Jesus said to him, "Judas, would you betray the Son of Man with a kiss?" 49 And when those who were around him saw what would follow, they said, "Lord, shall we strike with the sword?" 50 And one of them struck the servant of the high priest and cut off his right ear. 51 But Jesus said, "No more of this!" And he touched his ear and healed him. 52 Then Jesus said to the chief priests and officers of the temple and elders, who had come out against him, "Have you come out as against a robber, with swords and clubs? 53 When I was with you day after day in the temple, you did not lay hands on me. But this is your hour, and the power of darkness."

54 Then they seized him and led him away, bringing him into the high priest's house, and Peter was following at a distance. 55 And when they had kindled a fire in the middle of the courtyard and sat down together, Peter sat down among them. 56 Then a servant girl, seeing him as he sat in the light and looking closely at him, said, "This man also was with him." 57 But he denied it, saying, "Woman, I do not know him." 58 And a little later someone else saw him and said, "You also are one of them." But Peter said, "Man, I am not." 59 And after an interval of about an hour still another insisted, saying, "Certainly this man also was with him, for he too is a Galilean." 60 But Peter said, "Man, I do not know what you are talking about." And immediately, while he was still speaking, the rooster crowed. 61 And the Lord turned and looked at Peter. And Peter remembered the saying of the Lord, how he had said to him, "Before the rooster crows today, you will deny me three times." [62] And he went out and wept bitterly.

[63] Now the men who were holding Jesus in custody were mocking him as they beat him. [64] They also blindfolded him and kept asking him, "Prophesy! Who is it that struck you?" [65] And they said many other things against him, blaspheming him.

[66] When day came, the assembly of the elders of the people gathered together, both chief priests and scribes. And they led him away to their council, and they said, [67] "If you are the Christ, tell us." But he said to them, "If I tell you, you will not believe, [68] and if I ask you, you will not answer. [69] But from now on the Son of Man shall be seated at the right hand of the power of God." [70] So they all said, "Are you the Son of God, then?" And he said to them, "You say that I am." [71] Then they said, "What further testimony do we need? We have heard it ourselves from his own lips."

[23:13] Pilate then called together the chief priests and the rulers and the people, [14] and said to them, "You brought me this man as one who was misleading the people. And after examining him before you, behold, I did not find this man guilty of any of your charges against him. [15] Neither did Herod, for he sent him back to us. Look, nothing deserving death has been done by him. [16] I will therefore punish and release him."

[18] But they all cried out together, "Away with this man, and release to us Barabbas"— [19] a man who had been thrown into prison for an insurrection started

in the city and for murder. [20] Pilate addressed them once more, desiring to release Jesus, [21] but they kept shouting, "Crucify, crucify him!" [22] A third time he said to them, "Why, what evil has he done? I have found in him no guilt deserving death. I will therefore punish and release him." [23] But they were urgent, demanding with loud cries that he should be crucified. And their voices prevailed. [24] So Pilate decided that their demand should be granted. [25] He released the man who had been thrown into prison for insurrection and murder, for whom they asked, but he delivered Jesus over to their will.

[32] Two others, who were criminals, were led away to be put to death with him. [33] And when they came to the place that is called The Skull, there they crucified him, and the criminals, one on his right and one on his left. [34] And Jesus said, "Father, forgive them, for they know not what they do." And they cast lots to divide his garments. [35] And the people stood by, watching, but the rulers scoffed at him, saying, "He saved others; let him save himself, if he is the Christ of God, his Chosen One!" [36] The soldiers also mocked him, coming up and offering him sour wine [37] and saying, "If you are the King of the Jews, save yourself!" [38] There was also an inscription over him, "This is the King of the Jews."

[39] One of the criminals who were hanged railed at him, saying, "Are you not the Christ? Save yourself and us!" [40] But the other rebuked him, saying, "Do you not fear God, since you are under the same sentence of condemnation? [41] And we indeed justly, for we are receiving the due reward of our deeds; but this man has

done nothing wrong." ⁴² And he said, "Jesus, remember me when you come into your kingdom." ⁴³ And he said to him, "Truly, I say to you, today you will be with me in Paradise."

⁴⁴ It was now about the sixth hour, and there was darkness over the whole land until the ninth hour, ⁴⁵ while the sun's light failed. And the curtain of the temple was torn in two. ⁴⁶ Then Jesus, calling out with a loud voice, said, "Father, into your hands I commit my spirit!" And having said this he breathed his last. ⁴⁷ Now when the centurion saw what had taken place, he praised God, saying, "Certainly this man was innocent!" ⁴⁸ And all the crowds that had assembled for this spectacle, when they saw what had taken place, returned home beating their breasts. ⁴⁹ And all his acquaintances and the women who had followed him from Galilee stood at a distance watching these things.

COMMENTARY

Perhaps the most intriguing sporting spectacle to watch is the summer Olympics. It is played once every four years and viewers around the globe watch the world's best athletes compete against each other. Much of the drama, however, is with the athletes themselves. Most of them dedicate their entire existence—sacrificing a "normal" life—for this one event. Some of them crack under the pressure, while others excel. The drama is that no one really knows what will happen until the games begin. For Jesus, the time and place toward which He had directed His life was upon Him. Under unparalleled pressure before the cross (sweating drops of blood!)—Jesus succeeds. Yet, His victory was not just for Him. Rather, as His own disciples began to fail—cracking under the heaviness of the moment—Jesus prevailed on their behalf. They fail to pray—Jesus prays for them. As the injustice perpetrated against Jesus mounted, Jesus not only endured—He endured on behalf of those who were committing the crime! As He suffered on the cross, Jesus asked for forgiveness on behalf of those who nailed Him there. At every turn, Jesus fulfilled His vocation. He wasn't just a willing recipient of wrath; He was the very Lamb of God who, in a magnificent act of obedience and sacrifice, took away the sins of the world.

This passage begins with two distinct paths: on one we see Jesus' opponents finally put into motion the events that would lead to the death of this "annoying," would-be Messiah. What they had long hoped for gained popularity among the people—including one of Jesus' own disciples, Judas. Furthermore, those on this path assumed (correctly as it turned out), that if they could make the right charges against Jesus, then His followers could be just as easily persuaded to change sides. Easy come, easy go. Indeed this movement gained so much momentum that Jesus' most boisterous disciple, Peter, would wilt under the burden. This path had Satan—the ancient accuser himself—as its ultimate instigator and he would move toward getting all the important parties to accuse Jesus. The other path was led by Jesus. This path started with much fan-fare and the support of the common people. But the crowds were easily swayed and Jesus' path became less and less populated. By the end, only Jesus Himself would remain on this path.

Already in the city and knowing that the hour was near, Jesus called two of His disciples to make preparations for their Passover meal. While partaking in the Passover was sacred for any Jew, what was so important about that meal that Jesus deemed absolutely imperative? The Passover meal recalled the salvation that God had brought to Israel in Egypt by delivering her from the bonds of slavery. God told Moses that every firstborn in Egypt would be slain except those houses that had the blood of a lamb smeared on the doorposts. Those houses would be passed over and their firstborn spared. The next morning—after judgment had been executed—the Hebrews were released and had a pathway to freedom. The Passover meal then became a yearly remembrance of God's liberation of Israel from slavery.

Once Jesus had His disciples alone in the upper room He explained the Passover meal to them. The bread that He had broken for them would no longer recall the blood of a lamb that won Israel temporary freedom. Instead this bread was now His body which was to be broken for them. They would no longer look back and recall the freedom their nation once had, but would recall the blood of Jesus that won them lasting freedom. His blood would only need to be spilled once and in so doing He would provide a lasting means of salvation for all people everywhere (see Acts 17:30-33). Jesus was now the final Passover lamb, taking on Himself the judgment of God so that those who are in His family could be passed over and be led into freedom.

People thought Jesus' followers could be easily persuaded to turn against Him. How would the people around you classify you: devoted to the death or easily persuaded to turn against Jesus? Would they be right?

Look again at this Deuteronomy passage. Do you try to earn your way into God's blessings? If you're trying to achieve your own salvation, what does that say about Jesus' work at the cross?

Jesus' ministry to bring outsiders in, as we've seen throughout the Book of Luke, is highlighted once again at the Passover meal. The people of Israel were given a pattern of God's blessing that went like this: If you obeyed God's law you would receive a blessing and if you didn't you would receive a curse. As Deuteronomy 11:26-28 states, "See, I am setting before you today a blessing and a curse: the blessing, if you obey the commandments of the LORD your God, which I command you today, and the curse, if you do not obey the commandments of the LORD your God, but turn aside from the way that I am commanding you today, to go after other gods that you have not known." But now, Jesus shockingly put a twist to this way of blessing. His life demonstrated that He alone was deserving of God's blessings, yet, by His own will, He would instead receive the curse that all sinners—past, present, and future—deserved and He would absorb their judgment upon Himself on the cross. Likewise the blessing of His perfect life could be enjoyed by anyone through faith in Him.

Clearly His disciples were not ready to understand what Jesus was actually doing and preparing to endure. After the supper, Jesus' disciples showed that they did not understand what He was saying. They began a discussion about which of them was the greatest and who would have the most power when Jesus finally established His government. In response to this, Jesus told them they would have great power, but it would be exercised by service. There would be an alternative leadership style that would be characterized by sacrifice. Jesus Himself would soon provide the chief example of this.

After supper Jesus departed to go pray and in a moment alone He saw the cup of wrath that He would soon drink. He prayed that He would do His Father's will, no matter the cost. Soon afterward, Judas and a gang of officials approached to arrest Him. The moment had come and as Jesus noted, "This is the hour of darkness." From there He was passed from court to court, and in contrast to Peter who could not stand up to his accusers, Jesus boldly faced His opponents, putting them to shame. Yet, His fate would finally be in the hands of Pilate. who then placated the crowd. By then the masses were hungry for blood crying out, "Crucify Him." The crowd was given a choice to free a known murderer or to free Jesus, in whom Pilate could find no fault. The crowd demanded to free the murderer instead of Jesus. A guilty man would go free but an innocent man would die. If only all in the crowd knew that Jesus was not just doing this for Barabbas, but for all of them as well.

While on the cross, Jesus did two things that are vital in understanding His life. First, He cried out, "Father, forgive them" for those who were killing Him. This should tell us something about Jesus and His attitude toward those who hated Him. He didn't hate them back. He asked His Father to forgive them because they didn't know the depth of their actions. What does this teach Jesus' disciples about how to interact with those who disagree with them? Second, a criminal was being crucified on each side of Jesus. One criminal was repentant and acknowledged that he and the other criminal were receiving justice. He also recognized that Jesus was innocent and believed that somehow Jesus on a cross could have power to still bring in His Kingdom. So Jesus responded by assuring the criminal that indeed, today, he would be with Him and His Father in paradise.

Even in the last hour, Jesus was willing to listen to a repentant sinner. One who deserved to die for his crimes that day would be with Jesus in paradise. This shows us the nature of repentance and faith in Jesus. The criminal was remorseful and agreed with the judgment he was receiving. Nevertheless, he trusted in Jesus that He had the power to bring in His Kingdom and bring him—a confessed sinner—into it as well. Jesus at that last moment received this sinner and gave him the thing he always needed—real salvation.

> Jesus made Himself available in His last hour of life. How willing are you to do the same when in your last hour of patience? Convenience? Love? Is there ever a situation in which it's okay to shut yourself off from others?

HEADS UP!

At the heart of the mystery of human and divine interaction is the problem of evil. A classic example of this is the crucifixion of Jesus Himself. Jesus' death was at once a miscarriage of justice and the instruments of it were to be held accountable, while at the same time the exact same event was a part of God's plan. How can this be? Peter says this in Acts 2:23, "this Jesus, delivered up according to the definite plan and foreknowledge of God, you crucified and killed by the hands of lawless men." Individuals are culpable for their own actions, yet part of the divine mystery is that God uses their actions of evil to further His plans for good. Sometimes, as we have seen in the cross, God does this in surprising ways.

WARM-UP (10:00)

Have you ever prepared for something for a long time—perhaps even years? If so, what was the final test like? How would you describe yourself at test time?

SHOW SESSION 10 VIDEO: JESUS THE LAMB OF GOD (10:00)

In this video, Dr. Carson points out that the death of Jesus is a fulfillment of what was decreed throughout Scripture. The arrest happened after the Passover feast, but Jesus is the ultimate Passover lamb, sparing everyone who believes in Him. As a group, discuss the significance of the arrest occurring after the Passover feast as well as the new covenant that Jesus established through His death.

GROUP DISCUSSION (20:00)

We read in this session that Satan played a role in getting people to accuse Jesus, assuring His death on the cross. We can reason, then, that Satan actually contributed to God's plan to save the world. The next time you are convinced God is absent from your circumstances and Satan is taking control, what can you reason about God's plan?

Luke 22:15 says that Jesus "earnestly desired" to eat that last meal with His disciples. Is it surprising to you that the Son of God craved interaction with His human friends? Explain why or why not. When have you seen this in your own life?

Before Jesus' death on the cross, sacrifices were understood to elicit the favor of God. But now, God's blessing would be clearly established by grace. Why do you think many Christians seem to live by religion rather than relationship with God's Son?

Based on this scene with Pilate and the crowd, we know that sometimes God's will is, by our standards, unjust. How do you explain the gap between God's justice and our understanding of it?

_____

_____

_____

Throughout this study, we have seen Jesus grant salvation to many outsiders, but perhaps none quite as far outside as this criminal on the cross. What seems different about Jesus at the time He grants salvation to the criminal at His side? What does that tell you about His desire to save the lost?

_____

_____

_____

WRAP (10:00)

- Jesus was not just a willing recipient of wrath; He was the Lamb of God who, in a magnificent act of obedience and sacrifice, took away the sins of the world.

- Although Jesus was the only one deserving of God's blessings, He willingly received the curse that we all deserved. Because of this, the blessings of His perfect life can be enjoyed by anyone through faith in Him.

- Jesus never hated those who hated Him. Instead, He interceded for them and asked God to forgive them of their sins.

Close in prayer by asking God to bless each group member over the course of the week. Make time for the Take Home assignment below to enrich your experience with the Gospel of Luke.

TAKE HOME

This week, study Romans 3:21-26. What did Jesus' death on the cross actually accomplish?

JESUS AND THE VICTORY OF GOD'S SON

During His earthly life Jesus showed promise, but did His death on the cross mean that He failed? He healed the lame, raised the dead, and loved the lost, but He was overcome by evil and died shamefully on a cross. As any good Jew would know, to be hung on a cross and to die in front of one's enemies was a sure sign of God's curse (see Deut. 23:21; Gal. 3:13). To be hung on a "tree" was to be rejected by God—it was certainly no sign of being the Son of God! Or so all of His followers thought. After Jesus' crucifixion, two disciples were leaving Jerusalem feeling discouraged and distraught, their hopes for Jesus' messianic reign were dashed. Their attitude pictured what happened when other would-be messiahs had tasted death (see Acts 5:36-37). To be killed was interpreted as total failure and nothing could be done to change that. Nothing, that is, except One coming back to life, overcoming death itself! Only a resurrection from the dead could explain what happened next to Jesus' dejected disciples.

[1] But on the first day of the week, at early dawn, they went to the tomb, taking the spices they had prepared. [2] And they found the stone rolled away from the tomb, [3] but when they went in they did not find the body of the Lord Jesus. [4] While they were perplexed about this, behold, two men stood by them in dazzling apparel. [5] And as they were frightened and bowed their faces to the ground, the men said to them, "Why do you seek the living among the dead? [6] He is not here, but has risen. Remember how he told you, while he was still in Galilee, [7] that the Son of Man must be delivered into the hands of sinful men and be crucified and on the third day rise." [8] And they remembered his words, [9] and returning from the tomb they told all these things to the eleven and to all the rest. [10] Now it was Mary Magdalene and Joanna and Mary the mother of James and the other women with them who told these things to the apostles, [11] but these words seemed to them an idle tale, and they did not believe them. [12] But Peter rose and ran to the tomb; stooping and looking in, he saw the linen cloths by themselves; and he went home marveling at what had happened.

[13] That very day two of them were going to a village named Emmaus, about seven miles from Jerusalem, [14] and they were talking with each other about all these things that had happened. [15] While they were talking and discussing together, Jesus himself drew near and went with them. [16] But their eyes were kept from recognizing him. [17] And he said to them, "What is this conversation that you are holding with each other as

you walk?" And they stood still, looking sad.

¹⁸ Then one of them, named Cleopas, answered him, "Are you the only visitor to Jerusalem who does not know the things that have happened there in these days?" ¹⁹ And he said to them, "What things?" And they said to him, "Concerning Jesus of Nazareth, a man who was a prophet mighty in deed and word before God and all the people, ²⁰ and how our chief priests and rulers delivered him up to be condemned to death, and crucified him. ²¹ But we had hoped that he was the one to redeem Israel. Yes, and besides all this, it is now the third day since these things happened. ²² Moreover, some women of our company amazed us. They were at the tomb early in the morning, ²³ and when they did not find his body, they came back saying that they had even seen a vision of angels, who said that he was alive. ²⁴ Some of those who were with us went to the tomb and found it just as the women had said, but him they did not see." ²⁵ And he said to them, "O foolish ones, and slow of heart to believe all that the prophets have spoken! ²⁶ Was it not necessary that the Christ should suffer these things and enter into his glory?" ²⁷ And beginning with Moses and all the Prophets, he interpreted to them in all the Scriptures the things concerning himself.

²⁸ So they drew near to the village to which they were going. He acted as if he were going farther, ²⁹ but they urged him strongly, saying, "Stay with us, for it is toward evening and the day is now far spent." So he went in to stay with them. ³⁰ When he was at table with them, he took the bread and blessed and broke it and gave it to them. ³¹ And their eyes were opened, and they recognized him. And he vanished from their sight.

32 They said to each other, "Did not our hearts burn within us while he talked to us on the road, while he opened to us the Scriptures?"

33 And they rose that same hour and returned to Jerusalem. And they found the eleven and those who were with them gathered together,

34 saying, "The Lord has risen indeed, and has appeared to Simon!" 35 Then they told what had happened on the road, and how he was known to them in the breaking of the bread.

COMMENTARY

In years of doing pastoral counseling for couples and families I have observed something about persistent communication breakdowns: they never have anything to do with ears not functioning well. Rather, the breakdown happens when the listener refuses to hold off their expectation of what they think the other is saying and in so doing never really receive what is actually being said. By being convinced in their mind what the other is saying already, they miss an opportunity to learn what the other is truly saying. For three years Jesus had communicated to His disciples a straightforward message: He was going to be killed and would rise from the dead. Yet based on these accounts they clearly never understood Him.

A crucified messiah was simply a contradiction in terms, and Jesus' disciples couldn't get past their expectations of what a messiah ought to be like. Because of this, when Jesus was killed, they followed the same pattern of other Jewish revolutionary movements that had gone before them. There was one basic response to the death of a would-be messiah in ancient Judaism: quit the movement. When one's leader fell at the hands of the enemy, especially for all to see, the people saw it as a sign that God had publicly abandoned the leader. We see this pattern described in Acts 5:36-37: "Before these days Theudas rose up, claiming to be somebody, and a number of men, about four hundred, joined him. He was killed, and all who followed him were dispersed and came to nothing. After him Judas the Galilean rose up in the days of the census and drew away some of the people after him. He too perished, and all who followed him were scattered." The death would serve as a gauntlet that God was not behind this individual and was perhaps with some other leader instead. Hence one would never want to continue following a crucified messiah—that would have been pointless.

The two disciples on the road to Emmaus embody precisely what all of Jesus' followers were going through. They had high hopes that Jesus would be the One to redeem Israel, but they assumed now this was not going to happen. The fact that they were leaving Jerusalem meant they were convinced He was dead and not coming back. Indeed, the only thing that would change their minds would be if Jesus Himself would appear and explain what was really happening. That, as we have read, is exactly what happened next.

Jesus' response to the disciples' dejection was totally accurate: "O foolish ones." The word "foolish" here indicates someone who totally misunderstands a situation. What they thought was the final victory of evil over Jesus was, in reality, God's victory over evil, death, and the Devil.

The scope of Jesus' resurrection was more than anyone could fathom or prepare for. The women who came to Jesus' tomb fully expected to find Jesus' corpse there as the spices in their possession showed. The fact that Jesus told His disciples exactly what was going to happen did nothing to actually get them ready. How could they be ready to witness the event that would forever change the world? That their Jesus, who they walked and talked with over the course of three years, was the one who would not just reform Israel, but would redeem all humanity. That Jesus, whose mother they knew, had existed from before the beginning of time. That Jesus not only faced death with courage, but went through death and came out of the other side of it victorious!

How could His disciples be prepared to understand that Jesus, indeed, was cursed by God and that this was His plan all along? That on the cross, Jesus was not just a victim of an unjust verdict, but was a willing recipient of God's wrath on behalf of all sinners. The scope of Jesus' death and resurrection was just too big—their expectations and faith were just too small to take it in. For the two disciples on the road to Emmaus, Jesus explained all of this from the whole of the Scriptures. Every section of God's Word pointed to God's Son doing exactly what they had just witnessed.

When you feel as though Jesus is dead, absent from your life, are you more likely to cling hopefully to the promise that He lives, or give up, sad and dejected, like the disciples did? What helps you to realize He's walking right beside you?

Sometimes we just don't get God. Our faith and expectations are too small and we're frustrated that He isn't doing anything. How has God shown you that His ways are higher and better and greater than you thought?

Jesus' resurrection is the one and only way people can be saved. Who in your life is traveling a dead-end street and needs to hear the truth. Write as many names as you can think of and waste no time telling them about God's plan to save them through Jesus' death and resurrection?.

As Jesus ate with these two, He broke bread and then "their eyes were opened." This phrase echoes the very first meal mentioned in Scripture—Adam and Eve eating the fruit given to them by the serpent. They too had "their eyes opened," yet it was to the reality of sin and the curse that they had ushered into the world. Now for these two disciples, their eyes were opened, but not to the curse. Rather their eyes were opened to the final answer to the problem of the curse (see Gal. 3:13).

The only explanation for the origins of Christianity and its central message—that Jesus died and was raised to life—is that it is precisely what actually happened. This is the certainty that Luke promised to provide in the opening verses of his Gospel. The message was as shocking to them as it is to us today. The fact remains that this happened and we are all compelled to deal with the implications. As Paul would later proclaim, "The times of ignorance God overlooked, but know he commands all people everywhere to repent, because he has fixed a day on which he will judge the world in righteousness by a man whom he has appointed; and of this he has given assurance to all by raising him from the dead" (see Acts 17:30-31).

HEADS UP!

One of the questions Jesus' disciples had about His resurrection was understanding the exact nature of His physical body. What kind of body did He have? He could appear and disappear, but He could also eat. There was a continuity between His old body and His new body as His disciples could recognize Him and feel the wounds on His hands and feet. What Jesus experienced was not just resuscitation from the dead like what He had performed on others in His ministry. Instead what Jesus experienced was the long hoped for final resurrection. He was, as Paul would later describe, the first fruits from among the dead. In other words, when the New Testament talks about the "New Creation" (2 Cor. 5) and the redemption of world (see Romans 8) that will one day be experienced at the culmination of history, we can now look to Jesus as the first one to experience this new kind of physical existence.

WARM-UP (10:00)

Think of a time when a follower of Jesus, someone you really respected, failed in a very public way. How did it make you feel? How do you think Jesus' followers felt when Jesus died?

SHOW SESSION 11 VIDEO: JESUS AND THE VICTORY OF GOD'S SON (10:00)

In this video, Dr. Carson explains that no one expected the Messiah to be crucified like a condemned criminal. However, after Jesus' resurrection, He explained He had to be crucified and His resurrection was His vindication—He was fulfilling God's plan. As a group, discuss the passages of Scripture that Dr. Carson referenced that foretold the death and resurrection of Jesus (Isa. 53; Ps. 69). How do they point to victory?

GROUP DISCUSSION (20:00)

Perhaps you have considered it pointless to follow Jesus because He didn't come through the way you expected in a particular situation. Have you ever felt like "quitting the movement" of following Christ? Or seen others react in that way? What happened?

The women who visited the tomb brought spices with them. What does that tell us they believed about Jesus' death? How did their lives change when they saw otherwise?

According to Scripture, Jesus' absence from the tomb isn't the only proof He left as to His being alive. He went a step further by physically appearing multiple times to multiple people. Why do you think He went so far in proving His resurrection? Would you have been satisfied simply seeing an empty tomb, or would you have needed to see Jesus to believe Him? What finally convinced you of the truth?

Why do you think Jesus spent so much time explaining the Scriptures to the two disciples on the road to Emmaus rather than revealing Himself right away? What lessons can we learn from that approach? What do you think they felt when He opened their eyes to see that it was Him?

Take a few minutes to process the resurrection as though this is the first time you are hearing about it. Talk about what the resurrection meant for Jesus' followers at the time. What does it mean for your life?

WRAP (10:00)

- Jesus was God's victory over evil, death, and the Devil.

- Jesus was not a victim of an unjust verdict, but a willing recipient of God's wrath on behalf of all sinners.

- Jesus did not just experience resuscitation from the dead like He performed on others in His ministry. Jesus experienced the long hoped for final resurrection.

Close in prayer by asking God to bless each group member over the course of the week. Make time for the Take Home assignment below to enrich your experience with the Gospel of Luke.

TAKE HOME

Because this resurrection actually happened, what place does Jesus have over our lives? This week make a list of the implications of Jesus' resurrection and be ready to discuss it in next week's meeting.

NOTES

JOINING HIS MISSION

The disciples had just witnessed the event that would alter all of history by observing the undeniable mark of divine action. As His disciples would soon discover, however, Jesus didn't rise from the dead to just amaze His followers. The disciples themselves would be called into Jesus' mission. There was going to be more to the story. In many ways, for Jesus' disciples, their story was just beginning. Jesus was to send them into the world to proclaim that repentance and forgiveness of sins could be discovered through His death and resurrection. Jesus did not just come for Israel, but through His disciples, He was to go to the world. Jesus' focus on Jerusalem was not just because it is where He would die and rise from the dead, it was also because it would become the launching pad for His mission to the world. As He said in Acts 1:8, "But you will receive power when the Holy Spirit has come upon you, and you will be my witnesses in Jerusalem and in all Judea and Samaria, and to the end of the earth."

TEXT: LUKE 24:36-53

36 As they were talking about these things, Jesus himself stood among them, and said to them, "Peace to you!" 37 But they were startled and frightened and thought they saw a spirit. 38 And he said to them, "Why are you troubled, and why do doubts arise in your hearts? 39 See my hands and my feet, that it is I myself. Touch me, and see. For a spirit does not have flesh and bones as you see that I have." 40 And when he had said this, he showed them his hands and his feet. 41 And while they still disbelieved for joy and were marveling, he said to them, "Have you anything here to eat?" 42 They gave him a piece of broiled fish,43 and he took it and ate before them.

44 Then he said to them, "These are my words that I spoke to you while I was still with you, that everything written about me in the Law of Moses and the Prophets and the Psalms must be fulfilled." 45 Then he opened their minds to understand the Scriptures, 46 and said to them, "Thus it is written, that the Christ should suffer and on the third day rise from the dead, 47 and that repentance and forgiveness of sins should be proclaimed in his name to all nations, beginning from Jerusalem. 48 You are witnesses of these things. 49 And behold, I am sending the promise of my Father upon you. But stay in the city until you are clothed with power from on high."

50 Then he led them out as far as Bethany, and lifting up his hands he blessed them. 51 While he blessed them, he parted from them and was carried up into heaven.

⁵² And they worshiped him and returned to Jerusalem with great joy, ⁵³ and were continually in the temple blessing God.

COMMENTARY

Reading to my three young sons is one of the greatest joys in my life. Recently, we finished reading J.R.R. Tolkien's classic **The Hobbit** (before we watched the movie!). The story begins with a hobbit named Bilbo Baggins who was happily enjoying the simple pleasures of life. All that changed, however, when he was summoned to embark on an unexpected journey filled with adventure and risk. The most surprising aspect for Bilbo, it turned out, was not that he found himself on an adventure, but that he was strangely equipped for it. Indeed he discovered that his journey—rather mysteriously—was something he was called to. Many have a similar feeling with their experience with Jesus. They wanted a neat and clean life but an encounter with Jesus has called them into something much bigger than that.

For the disciples of Jesus, their hope was to see Jerusalem restored and have Israel freed from corruption on the inside and from oppression on the outside. Their hope was to have peace and quiet and live their lives. But with the resurrection of Jesus, His calling on their lives did not limit them to Israel, but opened their eyes to the world. Jerusalem was not going to be a restored safe haven for the saved, but it would become a launching pad for Jesus' global mandate. The steely focus that Jesus paid to Jerusalem was going to have a ricochet effect from that city to the rest of the world. As Luke described in Acts, just as Jesus had focused on Jerusalem, so too His disciples would focus on the ends of the earth represented by the world's most powerful city, Rome.

But first, His disciples needed to understand something about the Scriptures and something about power. Even though Jesus was risen from the dead and His disciples had touched His hands and feet, some still did not believe. Their minds and hearts did not have the ability to take in the reality before them. Besides giving them even more physical proof, He directed them to the Scriptures. Luke said He "opened their minds" so that they could understand the things written about Him in these Scriptures. Jesus broke down all the different parts of the Hebrew Bible—the Law of Moses, the Prophets, and the Psalms—which comprise the Old Testament in our Bibles today. In other words, a key to understanding Jesus is seeing that His life, death, and resurrection were, in fact, no surprise

Are you acting as an agent of repentance and forgiveness to the people around you, or would you say you are ignoring your mission altogether? Think of ways you can step out of your bubble this week and into the role Jesus has for you.

at all. Even though Jesus caught everyone off guard—the entire Old Testament pointed to Him! As Jesus once said to Bible experts, "you search the Scriptures because you think that in them you have eternal life; and it is they that bear witness about me" (John 5:39). One of the earliest practices of the church was not just witnessing the resurrection of Jesus, but explaining from the Scriptures that Jesus was the Messiah. "That Christ died for our sins in accordance with the Scriptures, that he was buried, that he was raised on the third day in accordance with the Scriptures" (1 Cor. 15:3-4).

In addition to understanding the Scriptures, they would also need the power of the same Spirit that had inspired those Scriptures. They would not be able to accomplish the mission that Jesus cast for them on their own—they would need a Helper. They would need to wait for the power of the Holy Spirit. The sending of the Spirit was itself prophesied in the Scriptures that stated, "I will pour out my Spirit on all flesh, and your sons and your daughters shall prophesy" (Joel 2:28; Acts 2:17). An important part of the message going from Jerusalem was having the Spirit empowering Jesus' messengers and having the Spirit at work in all types of people, including both Jews and Gentiles.

The message that Jesus' disciples would champion was "repentance and forgiveness of sins." The word repentance derived from an ancient Hebrew concept of "turn" or "return." It was a travel word used to describe a shift in direction from one destination to a quite different destination. This concept was then deepened to describe Israel's relationship with the Lord. Hence in the ministry of Jesus, when He talked about repentance He is talking about a fundamental re-orientation from one's own direction to that of Jesus. A part of the joy of this repentance is the experience of forgiveness that was a part of it. This reality is pictured beautifully by Jesus' story of the prodigal son. The fruit of the son's repentance, i.e. turning toward the father confessing his guilt, was the father's overwhelming grace and forgiveness. Hence the disciples would proclaim repentance and forgiveness but it would be—and this is the most important part—delivered "in His name." In other words, the entire message would be based on Jesus Himself. His life, death, and resurrection would be the foundation of this message and permeate every aspect of it.

WARM-UP (10:00)

Have you ever been on a real journey that was filled with adventure and danger? If so, what was it like?

SHOW VIDEO SESSION 12: JOINING HIS MISSION (10:00)

In this video, Dr. Carson explains that the followers of Jesus would become His witnesses to the nations. However, they would not be able to accomplish this mission alone. Though Jesus would not physically be with them any longer, He was sending the Holy Spirit to dwell in them. As a group, discuss the importance of the Holy Spirit and how the Spirit guides your life with regard to Christ's mission.

GROUP DISCUSSION (20:00)

Why didn't some disciples believe Jesus even after having physical proof of His resurrection? What do you think this tells us about the nature of doubt?

You've probably heard people say that the Old Testament became outdated or null after Jesus' death and resurrection. But what does Jesus say about it? How does that change the way you read it?

Why was it necessary for the disciples to wait on the power of the Spirit? After seeing Jesus' physical victory over death, do you think it was easy for them to wait? Explain.

If we need the Holy Spirit's involvement to do what Jesus has called us to, what does this tell us about the nature of this mission that we are called to?

_____

_____

_____

_____

WRAP (10:00)

- All of Scripture pointed to the death and resurrection of Jesus as Messiah.

- We cannot accomplish the mission that Jesus cast vision for on our own—we need a Helper.

- The disciples of Jesus should champion the message of repentance and forgiveness of sins.

Close in prayer by asking God to bless each group member over the course of the week. Make time for the Take Home assignment below to enrich your experience with the Gospel of Luke.

TAKE HOME

You are only half finished with Luke's contribution to the New Testament. Over the next couple of weeks, spend time reading his second volume, Acts. Pay attention as similar themes emerge during the early church's mission to the ends of the earth. What part do you feel God wants you to play in His universal mission?

_____

_____

_____

_____

NOTES

Welcome to Community!

Meeting together to study God's Word and experience life together is an exciting adventure. A small group is a group of people unwilling to settle for anything less than redemptive community.

CORE VALUES

COMMUNITY: God is relational, so He created us to live in relationship with Him and each other. Authentic community involves sharing life together and connecting on many levels with others in our group.

GROUP PROCESS: Developing authentic community takes time. It's a journey of sharing our stories with each other and learning together. Every healthy group goes through stages over a period of months or years. We begin with the birth of a new group, then deepen our relationships in the growth and development stages.

INTERACTIVE BIBLE STUDY: We need to deepen our understanding of God's Word. People learn and remember more as they wrestle with truth and learn from others. Bible discovery and group interaction enhance growth.

EXPERIENTIAL GROWTH: Beyond solely reading, studying, and dissecting the Bible, being a disciple of Christ involves reunifying knowledge with experience. We do this by taking questions to God, opening a dialogue with our hearts (instead of killing desire), and utilizing other ways to listen to God speak (other people, nature, art, movies, circumstances). Experiential growth is always grounded in the Bible as God's primary revelation and our ultimate truth-source.

POWER OF GOD: Processes and strategies will be ineffective unless we invite and embrace the presence and power of God. In order to experience community and growth, Jesus needs to be the centerpiece of our group experiences and the Holy Spirit must be at work.

REDEMPTIVE COMMUNITY: Healing best occurs within the context of community and relationships. It's vital to see ourselves through the eyes of others, share our stories, and ultimately find freedom from the secrets and lies that enslave our souls.

MISSION: God has invited us into a larger story with a great mission of setting captives free and healing the broken-hearted (Isaiah 61:1-2). However, we can only join in this mission to the degree that we've let Jesus bind up our wounds and set us free. Others will be attracted to an authentic redemptive community.

SHARING YOUR STORIES

The sessions in *The Gospel of Luke: From the Outside In* are designed to help you share a bit of your personal life with the other people in your group as you experience life together. Through your time together, each member of the group is encouraged to move from low risk, less personal sharing to higher risk communication. Real community will not develop apart from increasing intimacy over time.

HIGH RISK

HIGH RISK-TAKING BEHAVIOR

MEDIUM RISK-TAKING BEHAVIOR

LOW RISK-TAKING BEHAVIOR

Levels Of Sharing

NO RISK

BEGINNING —— Group Process ——→ **MATURING**

SHARING YOUR LIVES

As you share your lives together during this time, it's important to recognize that it's God who brought each person to this group, gifting the individuals to play a vital role in the group (1 Corinthians 12:1). Each of you was uniquely designed to contribute in your own unique way to building into the lives of the other people in your group. As you get to know one another better, consider the following four areas that will be unique for each person. These areas will help you get a "grip" on how you can better support others and how they can support you.

G - SPIRITUAL GIFTS:
God has given you unique spiritual gifts (1 Corinthians 12; Romans 12:3-8; Ephesians 4:1-16).

R - RESOURCES:
You have resources that perhaps only you can share, including skill, abilities, possessions, money, and time (Acts 2:44-47; Ecclesiastes 4:9-12).

I - INDIVIDUAL EXPERIENCES:
You have past experiences, both good and bad, that God can use to strengthen and encourage others (2 Corinthians 1:3-7; Romans 8:28).

P - PASSIONS:
There are things that excite and motivate you. God has given you those desires and passions to use for His purposes (Psalm 37:4,23; Proverbs 3:5-6,13-18).

To better understand how a group should function and develop in these four areas, consider taking your group on a journey in community using the LifeWay Small Groups study entitled *Great Beginnings*.

Leading a Small Group

You will find a great deal of helpful information in this section that will be crucial for success as you lead your group.

Reading through this section and utilizing the suggested principles and practices will greatly enhance the group experience. First is to accept the limitations of leadership. You cannot transform a life. You must lead your group to the Bible, the Holy Spirit, and the power of Christian community. By doing so your group will have all the tools necessary to draw closer to God and to each other, and to experience heart transformation.

MAKE THE FOLLOWING THINGS AVAILABLE AT EACH SESSION:

+ *The Gospel Of Luke: From the Outside In* book for each attendee
+ Extra Bibles
+ Snacks and refreshments (encourage everyone to bring something)
+ Pens or pencils for each attendee

THE SETTING AND GENERAL TIPS

#1   Prepare for each meeting by reviewing the material, praying for each group member, asking the Holy Spirit to join you, and making Jesus the centerpiece of every experience.

#2   Create the right environment by making sure chairs are arranged so each person can see every other attendee. Set the room temperature at 69 degrees. If meeting in a home, make sure pets are where they cannot interrupt the meeting. Request that cell phones be turned off unless someone is expecting an emergency call. Have music playing as people arrive (volume low enough for people to converse) and, if possible, burn a sweet-smelling candle.

#3   Try to have soft drinks and coffee available for early arrivals.

#4   Have someone with the spiritual gift of hospitality ready to make any new attendees feel welcome.

#5   Be sure there is adequate lighting so that everyone can read without straining.

#6   Think of ways to connect with group members away from group time. The amount of participation you have during your group meetings is directly related to the amount of time you connect with your group members away from the group meeting. Consider sending e-mails, texts, or social networking messages during the week encouraging them to come next week and to expect God to do great things throughout the course of this study.

#7   There are four types of questions used in each session: Observation (What is the passage telling us?), Interpretation (What does the passage mean?), Self-revelation (How am I doing in light of the truth unveiled?), and Application (Now that I know what I know, what will I do to integrate this truth into my life?). You may not be able to use all the questions in each study, but be sure to use some from each.

#8   Don't lose patience about the depth of relationship group members are experiencing. Building authentic Christian community takes time.

#9   Be sure pens or pencils are available for attendees at each meeting.

#10 Never ask someone to pray aloud without first asking their permission.

LEADING MEETINGS

#1   Before the Review sections, do not say, "Now we're going to do a review." The entire session should feel like a conversation from beginning to end, not a classroom experience.

#2   Be certain every member responds to the group questions. The goal is for every person to hear his or her own voice early in the meeting. People will then feel comfortable to converse later on. If members can't think of a response, let them know you'll come back to them after the others have spoken.

#3   Remember, a great group leader talks less than 10 percent of the time. If you ask a question and no one answers, just wait. If you create an environment where you fill the gaps of silence, the group will quickly learn they don't need to join you in the conversation.

#4   Don't be hesitant to call people by name as you ask them to respond to questions or to give their opinions. Be sensitive, but engage everyone in the conversation.

#5   Don't ask people to read aloud unless you have gotten their permission prior to the meeting. Feel free to ask for volunteers to read.

#6   Watch your time. If discussion extends past the time limits suggested, offer the option of pressing on into other discussions or continuing the current content into your next meeting.

REMEMBER: People and their needs are always more important than completing your agenda or finishing all the questions.